MILLION DOLLAR
MONEY SAVING SECRETS

*How to Keep More Of Your Hard Earned
Money And Become A Millionaire Faster*

JOHN C. MCKIBBON

Website: www.johnmckibbon.com

Order this book online at www.trafford.com
or email orders@trafford.com

Most Trafford titles are also available at major online book retailers.

Note for Librarians: A cataloguing record for this book is available from Library and Archives Canada at www.collectionscanada.ca/amicus/index-e.html

Printed in Victoria, BC, Canada.

ISBN: 978-1-4269-1088-3 (sc)

We at Trafford believe that it is the responsibility of us all, as both individuals and corporations, to make choices that are environmentally and socially sound. You, in turn, are supporting this responsible conduct each time you purchase a Trafford book, or make use of our publishing services. To find out how you are helping, please visit www.trafford.com/responsiblepublishing.html

Our mission is to efficiently provide the world's finest, most comprehensive book publishing service, enabling every author to experience success. To find out how to publish your book, your way, and have it available worldwide, visit us online at www.trafford.com

Trafford rev. 6/10/2009

Trafford PUBLISHING® www.trafford.com

North America & international
toll-free: 1 888 232 4444 (USA & Canada)
phone: 250 383 6864 ♦ fax: 250 383 6804 ♦ email: info@trafford.com

The United Kingdom & Europe
phone: +44 (0)1865 487 395 ♦ local rate: 0845 230 9601
facsimile: +44 (0)1865 481 507 ♦ email: info.uk@trafford.com

DEDICATION

This book is dedicated to Susan, my wife for having the patience and under-standing while I spent hours, days, weeks and months writing this book and at all times giving me encouragement to continue.

AUTHOR'S NOTE

The material in this publication is provided for information purposes only. It is designed to provide accurate and authoritative information on the subject of personal finance, mortgages, credit card usage, and how to negotiate a better price or terms. In order to make this information real I have provide examples wherein the facts are true and as accurate as possible but I have changed the names to protect the privacy of the individuals. It is sold with the understanding that neither the author nor the publisher is engaged in rendering legal, financial advice, accounting or other professional services by publishing this book. Laws, regulations and procedures are under constant change and therefore all examples shown or given are intended for general guideline use only. The author and publisher specifically disclaim any liability, loss, or for that matter risk which is incurred as a consequence, directly or indirectly, of the use and application of any of the contents of this work. Since each person's financial situation is unique, questions that involve you are best to be addressed to the appropriate professional. It is strongly recommended that you get legal, accounting, tax, financial and insurance advice from the appropriate professional before acting on any information contained in this book.

WEBSITE: www.johnmckibbon.com

CONTENTS

❖

Introduction

Y ou are going to love this book. The time you invest in this book will be a tremendously exciting, rewarding and fast-paced learning experience for you. Now, let's get started.

Have you ever heard the phrase "money is the root of all evil?" To be accurate, "Money is not the root of all evil; the love of money is the root of all evil."

History Of Money

Money was originally developed in order to allow people to purchase products or services with something of value that could be used by more than just the person receiving the product or service. In other words the receiver could keep it or give it to other people for their product or service.

At one time everything was bartered. If you wanted a product or service from someone else, you simply exchanged something that you owned, or you provided a service for the person who had what you wanted.

The system worked well; but only if what they owned and what you owned was what both of you wanted.

Many times it didn't work; therefore it was necessary to come up with a way so that you could get what you wanted, in exchange for something the other person wanted. It needed to be something that the person you traded with, could take it and trade it, with another person. By doing this you could get a product or service from that other person, not just now; but in the future.

Hence, cultures around the world at different times in their civilized development developed a coin to be used as money. These coins were made from gold, silver, bronze, copper etc. It wasn't always coin but it was always something that was not readily available to everyone. In Canada for example original coin was in fact a bracelet that was made by the Indians, this bracelet was difficult to make and it took a considerable amount of time to make, but because of the detail and rarity of the bracelet, it too qualified as something that could be used as money.

Why is the coin made from rare metals?

If coinage were made from something that everyone could get easily, it would be of little value.

Gold and silver were used for the more valuable coins, but soon it was realized other coins were needed. Coins that were not as valuable, in order to make change when the coins value was greater than the service or product being provided. They started to use metals that were not as valuable, such as copper, nickel, bronze etc.

When paper money was originally issued by most countries around the world it was backed by gold, and this gold was kept on deposit, in government vaults. The term dollar originally meant that its value was 1/20th of an ounce of gold and the United States remained on a fairly strict gold standard until 1914. For years people took their gold to banks and received coins or what was called gold receipt as "currency."

As time passed the gold receipts became commonplace and people started to refer to them as "dollars", to carry around, as gold was heavy and awkward.

Governments began to print notes, "dollars" which were referred to as currency and established a system whereby gold was exchanged for government currency.

Today however, this is no longer the case as currency is printed and seems to flow regardless of the future consequences of the debt load and gold is no longer placed in the vault to back up the currency. In many of the countries today, printed money is only backed by the governments' word that they have the ability and assets to stand behind all the printed money they have issued. Pretty scary thought.

Before the onslaught of credit cards, the local storeowners gave credit. The storeowners also referred to as merchants would extend credit to their customers until their customers were either paid by their employer or until their customers sold their crops, furs, eggs etc. and would repay the merchant.

Originally credit was given interest free, regardless of how long it took you to pay the amount owing, (within reason) but alas, such is no longer the case. There were no credit bureaus then, so a merchant's only recourse if you did not pay up was to let the other local merchants know of your bad paying habits.

Personal credit, for the most part today is provided on a credit card and most cards typically, allow a 21-day grace period. To avoid interest charges you must pay the balance owing, on the account in full, within the grace period, otherwise you will be charged interest.

Businesses still extend credit to other credit worthy businesses for a period of time. Most often, the credit terms are for a period of 30 to 60 days. Failure to pay within this time frame usually results in an interest charge added to the amount owing

If you borrow money, buy product or receive a service and you do not pay the bill when due a creditor can seek legal action to get paid. They will add interest, penalties, legal and other charges to the original amount and these extra charges can cost you as much or more than the original amount.

Banks and other businesses get their money by paying others for depositing their money with them or by issuing bonds, stocks etc. The details of exactly what takes place to make this happen is beyond the scope of this book but let me say this, once they have the money they loan it to other businesses or to individuals at a higher rate of interest then they pay.

First Job

Do you remember your first job? I remember mine and how excited I was. I'll bet you were too. Just knowing you would have your own money, to spend on anything you wanted. You bought the clothes you wanted, went to the cinema when you wanted, bought your own music,

CD's, DVD's and videos. It felt so good to be able to buy whatever you wanted.

When you turned 18, I'll bet the credit card companies were beating a path to your door to get you to use their credit cards. They offered free gifts, extended terms and introductory low rates of interest. Heck, they didn't mind that you were only working part time while going to school. They welcomed you to the world of credit card users.

CHAPTER 1

❖

Legacy

Let's talk for a minute about something few people ever give much thought to and that is "What legacy do you want to leave your children?"

When children first arrive in this world what is it that most parents want for them to have besides food, shelter, and clothing?

Most parents want to give their children the best education possible; so that when they finish school they can get the best job possible.

They teach them right from wrong so that they can get along with other people, manners and their family values and principles. The list of values is too numerous to list, but the bottom line is parents want their children to have a better life than have.

This is absolutely without a doubt, a wonderful thought.

So let me ask you, if this is what most people want then why are so many people doing so little to get out of debt? Are you willing to give your children, your financial burden?

What financial burden?

The burden that will require your children to care for you financially when you are elderly and in need of a place to live, medication, health care or enough food for as long as you live. You and I know we can't rely on our government to provide for us.

❖

CHAPTER 2

Positive Attitude

Positive Attitude

I believe that it is extremely important to be positive in your outlook on life.

"Choose To Be Happy"

Having the can do attitude in life will take you a long way. And along the way, you will enjoy a happier richer life. We do truly become what we think about most of the time. Our sub-conscious mind is amazingly powerful, so powerful in fact that it is actually reaching to forces in the universe that can't be explained at this time.

The two most emotionally vulnerable times for us are when we start to go to sleep and when we wake up. The emotions we have at these times tend to set our mood and get our subconscious mind working for us.

Your subconscious mind, does not know the difference between what is real and what is imaginary. We can easily trick our mind. Good or bad! So, think good positive thoughts about the outcome for the day and avoid at all cost the negative thoughts. Don't walk away from negative people "run away!"

As children we don't know the meaning of failure but as we grow we are taught by our parents, teachers and even our friends that failure is a bad thing that must be avoided at all cost. I totally disagree with this thought. If we don't fail at anything it only means that we are not trying anything new.

Increase the number of times you fail and you will surely become more successful. Give up and do nothing, will get you exactly that; nothing.

CHAPTER 3

❖

Wealth Accumulation

J ust about everyone in the world wants to accumulate wealth. I am sure you
do or you wouldn't be reading this book. However, in order to achieve the
financial success you want you must become financially savvy. The sad fact is
that only about 1 person in 3000 is financially savvy.

Why is this?

Financial savvy is not taught in grade schools, high schools, colleges or
universities as a general course. It is only available as a specialty subject.
Parents are so busy with their own money woes that they don't have time
to involve their children in what it means to earn and pay interest and how
stressful it is to make ends meet. What a shame this is, when you consider the
fact that the average person spends their working life helping someone else
get rich and they do it in many cases for a mere pittance.

Our education system does not teach our children how to achieve their
dreams; it does not give them real life lessons on the best way to handle
money. The school system teaches our children to rely on others, it is a system that trains our children, how to work as employees, not entrepreneurs.

I realize that not everyone wants to be, or is capable to be an entrepre-
neur but if you were not taught the basics in school how would you know?
Perhaps if you had been taught the basics, you would at least understand
more of what it takes to own your own business.

After working a lifetime, many people get to retire but only a fortunate few will retire and live comfortably.

Most people in North America have assets that on average, if sold would not give them enough for a two-week vacation in Europe. In fact to add insult to injury, it would not be enough to pay off their credit card debt. Pretty scary if you ask me!

So what is it you can do about it? For starters read this book, not just once, but two or maybe even three times and start acting on the knowledge you get from it right away.

Don't wait until the third reading. Start now!

Much of what I say will be different than what you may have already been taught and exposed to. You may not always agree with what I say, so be it. But it works, so disagree and then do it anyway.

"Winners do what losers are unwilling to do without being told to do it!"

Advice From Other People

Learn to listen and consider other people's advice, but also learn to evaluate the advice to be sure it fits within your life goals. Do not blindly follow the advice you get from relatives, friends, bankers, stockbrokers and politicians. Especially the politicians!

Government bureaucrats and bankers would have you believe that you can spend yourself to wealth.

They want you to rack up even more debt by buying a new car, a bigger house, new furniture etc. You cannot spend yourself to wealth but you can spend yourself to the poor house, which will result in bankruptcy. "The secret to becoming a millionaire is simply **spending less than you earn and investing more in you.**"

A simple example is the sub-prime mess and credit default swaps the United States and many other countries have gotten into.

How did this happen?

It happened because lenders loaned money to people who could not afford to pay the loan back. Yes, they were able to make the payments when low introductory interest rates were in effect, but when the introductory period was over the interest would go up and these poor souls could not pay the new payment. They had no idea what they were a getting themselves into.

Most people place bankers on a pedestal. They do this because they believe the bankers are better educated in the handling of money. Bankers can be very intimidating because these are the people that can say yes or no to your loan request. With this trust in bankers most people have believed, that if the banker said they could afford to buy their own home that they must be able to buy it.

If these people had been taught just a few things from this book and practiced what I am teaching, they would have lived within their means. Now all of us will pay for many years into the future to get this mess cleaned up but cleaned up it will get.

"Spend Less Than You Earn"

This is real simple and all it requires to be successful is discipline. The majority of people spend far more than they earn. Don't spend more than you earn, invest in you first and as soon as you can, get out of debt. I also recommend that as soon as you can afford it, that you give a portion of your earnings to a charity of your choice, as there are so many needy people in the world that can use your help.

Invest in You

I believe the two most important investments in you that you should make are to continue a life of learning. Education is not a destination; it is a journey. Invest in your knowledge as it will grow and last you forever. You can lose money and even go broke. But with knowledge, you can start again. Many successful entrepreneurs went broke and some more then once. They learned from it and went on to do better the next time.

The sad fact is less than 10% of the population ever read another book after they have finished their formal education. Continuously invest in your knowledge by reading at least one hour every day in any subject you like and after 3-years you will become proficient in that subject and after 5-years you will be an expert in that subject.

Attend good seminars and trade shows in your chosen field of interest and as often as you can, preferably 4 to 5 times a year. Instead of listening to the radio, turn your car into a university on wheels and listen to educational material. I must warn you that if you are driving, do not attempt to do anything that may distract you and result in an accident.

Just listen and learn!

The second investment you must make is in your health. Eat a good balanced diet and get plenty of exercise. Walking 3 to 4 times a week for thirty minutes will give you more, energy; more self-confidence and you will feel better and live a healthier life.

Debt

I cannot emphasize this enough; debt will keep you poor and the banks rich. Avoid it like a deadly disease. Like a disease it will keep eating at you and eventually sink you in a mire of debt. You will be far better off if you wait and pay cash for what it is you want.

This is especially true when it comes to buying an automobile. In most cases a car is one of the worst investments you could ever make. Cars are expenses and costly ones at that, they are not investments. Depreciation on a new car can cost you up to 50% of its value in the first year you own it.

Cut Up The Credit Cards

Cut up all but one credit card as soon as you can. Credit cards will keep you broke since you must pay 18 to 26% in interest charges. With high interest charges, it's no wonder most people stay in debt and never get the balance owing paid off.

Pay Yourself First

What does this mean? It means that you start saving at least 10% of whatever you earn. Every time your employer pays you, you must take at least 10% of the money and invest it for you. The best way to do this is before you get your hands on the money have it deposited directly into a high interest paying savings account.

I know what you're going to say as I have heard it many times before. "I can't do it. I barely get by now." There just isn't enough money. I take pop bottles back to the store to get enough money for food...and on and on.

Trust me when I say that anything worthwhile is worth struggling for. I am not asking you to invest more than 10%, although more would be better.

Let's start by me giving you a real life analogy. If your employer were to tell you today that business was slow and times were tough and starting next week, she will be cutting your earnings by 10%

What would you do? Would you be upset? Of course you would be upset. Would you quit? I doubt it. Besides quitting is not an option, at least not without another job to go to. Especially if you are up to your eyeballs in debt, or worse it is the only job you have training and experience with.

Most people would complain, but they would accept it, and life would go on. I don't want you to fit the mold of most people. I want you to be one of the select few, who have options.

How do you get options? You get options by setting a money goal and by developing the mindset that you come first. This is not selfishness. It is reality. If you don't look after you, then how can you look after anyone else?

If you can't start with 10% then start with 5% and make a commitment, in writing to yourself, that you will increase this percentage at 1 % increments, starting on certain date, a date set by you. Why commit in writing? Studies have shown time and again that only 3 % of the population put their goals in writing and those who do put them in writing are the ones who are the most successful at achieving them. If it's not in writing it's merely a wish.

The best way to increase the amount of money that you pay to you is to increase it whenever you get a raise from your employer or when the payroll tax rates change and you notice a small increase in your pay.

I'll bet that once the process of automatically paying yourself first starts, and you start to see your money grow, thanks to compound interest, (*Albert Einstein called it the eighth wonder of the world*) you will want to contribute more.

Cutting back on your spending habits will not be easy and I know there will be times when you will feel like you are running up the side of a mountain, a mountain that seems to go on forever and you can't see the top. Trust me its there; but you can't see it, yet.

There is a way to end the mountain climbing and I will show you how. First you must start living within your means and you need to start the automatic cycle of investing 10% of your earnings in you. By setting it up as an automatic saving program, you have less temptation to spend it.

You need to set up a program, where 90% of your money, is deposited in your spending account (this is the account you use to pay your expenses), including debts and the other 10% gets paid to you and it is deposited automatically into a high interest paying savings account.

Talk to your employer about making these deposits automatic. If they are unable or unwilling to do it, then arrange for your bank to do it automatically for you. By doing it automatically you are protecting yourself from yourself. "It is not how much you earn…its how much you learn to keep."

"Spend less than you earn."

"The Mind doesn't listen until the heart gives its permission."

Before you do or buy anything, you first want it in your heart, and then your conscious mind will justify it to you. To get what you want in life, first get your subconscious mind, working on how it will get it for you, legally and in a realistic time frame, a time frame you have selected.

"There are no limitations to the mind except those we acknowledge; both poverty and riches are the offspring of thought." Napoleon Hill.

"If you believe you can or believe you can not you are right." Henry Ford

You must have a financial plan. This plan needs to be both short term and long term. At the end of every month, plan your next month's savings and expenses. We already covered part of the long-term plan by paying yourself first.

By paying yourself first you are taking the first step of the long-term plan. However, it has been proven that those who review their past month or better still week's expenses is more apt to save more in the following week or month.

Why?

Many times when a goal or objective is set too far into the future people do not save near as much as they do when they also plan for the short term.

Your financial plan must include more than just savings; it must be a combination of many different strategies. In the plan be sure to include budgeting, credit card debt, other debt, buying, negotiating and how you will build your emergency fund. Don't worry if you are unsure how to do this. By the time you finish this book you will be able to do it with ease.

CHAPTER 4

❖

Canada Tax Free
Savings Account (TSFA)

O n January 1, 2009, Canada started a Tax Free Savings Account (TFSA). The purpose of which is to allow Canadians to invest money tax free in a TFSA, up to a contribution maximum of $5,000.00 in 2009. In the last chapter we spoke about paying "you first." This TFSA is the perfect place to start. By the time you have finished this chapter you will understand why.

Any Canadian individual (other than a trust) who is a resident of Canada, and is 18 years of age or older and has a Social Insurance Number (SIN) is eligible to start a TFSA plan.

The contribution limit has been set at $5,000.00 for 2009. It is not necessary to contribute the full amount you may if you can afford it. But if you don't contribute the maximum, any shortfall to the maximum allowable contribution of $5,000.00 is carried forward indefinitely. What this means is if you contribute $1,000.00 in 2009 you will still have a carried forward contribution room amount of $4,000.00 to use in future years.

The maximum amount will be reviewed on an annual basis and it is indexed to the inflation rate. The indexed amount provided, will be rounded to the nearest $500.00 increments. For example, assuming that, in 2009, 2010 and 2011 the inflation rate is 2 %, the TFSA dollar limit would remain at $5,000.00 for the 2010 and 2011 year and it will increase to $5,500.00 in 2012.

You can invest this money in the same way you now invest RRSP money. That is you can invest it in interest income, bonds, dividends and capital gains. Keep in mind though that unlike a Registered Retirement Savings Plan (RRSP) contribution, any contribution, to the TFSA is not tax deductible and therefore, is not an allowable deduction, from your income. Also note, withdrawals from an RRSP are taxable but withdrawals from your TFSA are not taxable.

In order to contribute to an RRSP you need to earn income, not so with this plan, you can contribute up to the maximum allowable contribution room and it is available for all individuals who meet the criteria outlined in paragraph 2, of this chapter, regardless of annual income or net worth.

You can withdraw money from your TFSA at any time without ever having to pay tax on the money withdrawn and without affecting your eligibility for federal income tested benefits and credits. Other benefits such as the old age security (OAS) benefits, guaranteed income supplement (GIS) or employment insurance (EI) benefits are not affected and it does not affect your eligibility for the goods and services tax (GSTC) the working income tax benefit (WITB) the Canada child tax benefit (CCTB) or the age credit.

If you do withdraw money from the TFSA the withdrawal will not reduce your contribution room for that year but if you have contributed your maximum allowable contribution for the year and make a withdrawal, you will not be allowed to put the money back into your TFSA during that year, unless you are willing to pay a monthly tax equal to 1 % of the highest excess amount in the month, for each month you are in an over contribution position.

You will be allowed to put the money you withdrew, back into the TFSA in a subsequent year because the subsequent year's contribution limit will be increased by the amount you withdrew.

TFSA Example: In 2009, Patricia contributed $5,000.00 in a TFSA. Shortly after she made the contribution she withdrew $2,000.00 to buy an antique car. Unfortunately, the antique car she wanted was no longer available. Since the car was not available, Patricia wanted to put the money back into her TFSA. However, since she had used up her contribution room for 2009 it would be subject to the above mentioned tax penalty.

TFSA Example Continued: Patricia's $2,000.00 withdrawal can be put back in 2010, because her 2009 withdrawal gets added to her available contribution room in 2010.

2010 - Contribution room   = $5,000.00

2010 - Eligible withdraw in 2009 =   2,000.00

Total - TFSA room in 2010   = $7,000.00

The money for the TFSA can come from sources such as your spouse, common law partner, child, father, mother, brother or sister without triggering the attribution rule under the income tax act. I won't explain the attribution rule in this book but let me again point out that you do not need to earn the money to be eligible to contribute to a TFSA, the money may come from any legal source and from anyone.

There may come a time when you need to withdraw the money from your TFSA; but instead of withdrawing the money you may be in a better position to get a loan from your financial institution and use the TFSA as collateral. By using the TFSA as collateral, you should get a preferred loan rate and if this rate is lower than you are earning on your investments it may be a very prudent thing to do. However, unless you will earn more by using the banks money I don't recommend you borrow.

You may however; want to borrow if you are caught in the situation where the value of your investments, in stocks or bonds is depressed and you don't want to sell those investments while there values are depressed. (Speak with your financial advisor)

I pointed out in the first paragraph of this chapter how useful a TFSA could be as part of your "pay you first" program. In fact you could if necessary use the TFSA, as your emergency fund. Please read the chapters on paying yourself first and on emergency funds.

The "pay you first" fund is intended to build money, money that you will keep until you retire or until you must use it; but use it, only in an absolute emergency. If you cannot afford to "pay you first" and build an emergency fund, then use your "pay you first money" to start building your emergency fund. Never stop paying yourself first and as soon as you have enough in the emergency fund stop putting more into it; but do continue paying yourself first.

How To Set Up A Tax Free Savings Account (TFSA)

You can set up a TFSA through a bank, credit union or other financial service provider who is eligible to issue a TFSA. They are referred to as the issuer of the plan.

As the TFSA holder you will need to provide to the issuer your Social Insurance Number (SIN), your date of birth, and your address of residence, so that they may register your qualifying arrangement as a TFSA. Failure to provide this information or providing incorrect information may cause the registration of the TFSA to be denied, resulting in possible tax consequences.

You are allowed to have more than one TFSA at the same time, as long as the total amount of all contributions during the year does not exceed your TFSA contribution room for that year.

You are also allowed to set up a self directed TFSA if you prefer to build and manage your own investment portfolio by buying and selling a variety of different investments.

CHAPTER 5

❖

Emergency Money

Having emergency money must be near the top of your list of goals. I know it won't be possible for you to do everything at the same time. This means that you need to prioritize your goals.

You must get a handle on your daily, weekly and monthly expenses. From here the next step is to start paying down any credit card balances and outstanding loans.

I will discuss credit card debt and just how much it is costing you in interest in more detail in a later chapter.

Once you start reducing the amount you owe on your credit cards you will notice that you will have more credit available to you on your card. Do not use this available credit, unless you have absolutely no other choice. It is not there for you to buy anything else. It will be the cushion you need to fund an emergency if you have no other choice.

As soon as your loans are paid in full, start putting money away in your emergency fund.

Why?

Because this money can be used for those unexpected emergency expenses that occasionally come along. And as you know, they always come along when we least expect them. Expenses such as a pay cut or a loss of job or a major car or home repair.

I recommend that you plan to put enough money in this fund to pay all your expenses for a minimum period of 3-months but preferably 6-months. This means that if you had no money coming to you because of a job loss or a disability you would still be able to pay all expenses for this period.

I know building an emergency fund such as this may take you a few years; but once you do, you will live life with a lot less stress. Just think, if you lost your job knowing you have enough money to last you at least 6-months will relieve plenty of stress. During this time you could find another job and get back on your feet.

Who knows what the emergency might be; but one thing is certain with a 6-month cash reserve you will be in a much better position to handle it.

❖

CHAPTER 6

Canada Deposit Insurance

The Canada Deposit Insurance Corporation (CDIC) is a federal Crown corporation created by Parliament, and its purpose is to insure Canadians savings in case their bank or other CDIC member institution fails or goes bankrupt. CDIC is not a bank nor is it an insurance company and you do not need to pay a fee or sign up for anything as they insure most savings automatically.

How does the CDIC earn their money?

They earn it by charging the banks and other financial institutions who are members a premium.

How do you know if your institution is covered? Visit the CDIC on line @ www.cdic.ca and click on the caption at the top left side "Where are My Savings Insured by CDIC." The CDIC insures your money in up to 6 different categories. So it is possible to have up to $100,000.00 in each category. You can have all 6 categories at a different financial institution not a different branch but at a different institution and you will be insured.

Before I list the categories it is important for you to remember this main point; the CDIC does not insure U.S. dollars and foreign currency on deposit. Only Canadian currency.

It does not insure mutual funds and stocks and it does not insure anything in a term longer than 5-years

Categories

Savings held in one name
Savings held in more than one name.
Savings held in trust.
Savings held in an RRSP.
Savings held in a RRIF.
Savings held for paying reality taxes on mortgage payments.

Category Example

If you have your funds deposited at a CDIC member institution and the breakdown is as follows you are insured.

Category 1 – you have $90,000.00 on deposit.
and

Category 2 – you have $20,000.00 on deposit
and

Category 3 – you have $50,000.00 in a 4-year GIC
and

Category 4 – you have $30,000.00 in an RRSP

All are fully insured, if the institution where you have these funds were to go bankrupt the CDIC would reimburse you $190,000.00.

CHAPTER 7

❖

United States of America Deposit Insurance

The Federal Deposit Insurance Corporation (FDIC) is a United States government corporation. It provides deposit insurance that guarantees checking and savings deposits in member banks, currently up to $250,000.00 per depositor bank.

This is a temporary amount that has been put in place to give you a depositor a comfort level during the present financial crises. On January 1, 2010 the amount will be lowered back to $100,000.00 for all deposit categories except IRA's and certain retirement accounts that will continue to be insured up to $250,000.00 per owner.

The FDIC insurance covers accounts at different banks separately not branches. For example if you have $500,000.00 and deposit this money at two different banks, you are insured for the $500,000.00.

Also, accounts in different ownerships such as beneficial ownership, trusts, and joint accounts are considered separately for the $250,000.00 limit. The FDIC act of 2005 covers your individual retirement account up to $250,000.00.

CHAPTER 8

Instant Gratification

I know many of you will have a hard time believing me when I say "you will be better off in the long run, if you just learn to live within your means."

At a young age we learn that it feels better to have it now, rather than wait. I don't believe it is better to have it now, yes; instant gratification is a good short-term solution. As a child you didn't have to concern yourself and worry about how it would get paid, since you weren't the one paying for it.

Owing money, when you don't have the money to pay for what you bought is very stressful. Would it not be better if you had the financial freedom to do as you wish, when you wish?

It is not easy to cut back spending money when you are constantly bombarded with advertisements to buy this or buy that. Why do most people give in to these ads and buy things that they don't really need? Because, they believe it will give them the satisfaction and the happiness that they need, and for a while it does.

In most cases the satisfaction is short lived, because when it comes time to pay the bill, most people do not have the money, and this leads to stress. A sad fact is, more people are using their credit cards, in order to pay their monthly expenses.

When you spend everything you earn, or worse more than you earn, you sentence yourself to a life of uncertainty and stress. If you spend more than you earn you will never reach your goal of financial freedom.

You must learn to live within your means and "**spend less than you earn.**"

I know people, as I am sure you do who earn a great deal of money and dine at the finest restaurants, wearing the nicest clothes, driving a luxury automobile, perhaps they own a boat and the big house but at the end of the day they are not happy and can't understand why.

They are stressed with trying to keep up with their expensive lifestyle and yet they can't imagine a simpler life, without these luxuries. Luxuries are great; but remember it is not how much you earn but how much you keep.

How To Get Control of Your Spending

Now that you have decided to set aside 10% for you, let's see how you can find some money, by cutting your spending habits. Spending habits that you now have and will be better off without.

This is easier said then done. Fighting those urges when you go shopping, to buy that new outfit, stereo, etc. We buy with our heart, and we justify it, with the mind (logic).

Purchases don't even have to be for large items, smaller purchases for coffee or muffins eat away at your money without you realizing it.

By cutting back on these smaller purchases, it will help you to become a millionaire sooner and help you to retire to a richer stress free life.

I would like you to track for the next month, everything you spend your money on and I do mean everything. Coffee, snacks, lunch and dinner. Write down how many times a week you eat out. Write down the cost of those specialty coffees and the cost of the cinnamon bun, muffin, donut etc.

Write it all down!
I'll bet you can cut your monthly costs by 10% and you will barely notice the cut.
OK!
At first you might notice it a little; but I'll bet that within 21 days you will wonder how and why you ever spent so much for so little satisfaction. (*See appendix for sample form*)

I'll bet you can easily come up with $15.00 a day and that's just a start. If you invested $15.00 a day, deposited it semi-monthly and it earned a 7% return compounded semi-monthly you will have at the end of:

1 year	=	$5,907.27
2 years	=	11,997.58
3 years	=	18,528.82
5 years	=	33,044.10
10 years	=	79,588.47
15 years	=	145,604.44
20 years	=	239,237.84
30 years	=	560,404.81
40 years	=	1,206,497.04

If you are married or have a significant other in your life you could double the rate of savings and double the investment income you will earn over the same period.

Small things will help you to become a millionaire but not alone, Couple these small things with my ideas from this book and you will get you there, sooner than you think. Before I begin the chapter on credit cards, I want to give you a few tips on what to do before you go shopping.

"Spend Less Than You Earn"

First:
Don't allow yourself to get caught up in the emotion of the crowd, especially at holiday time or when there are gigantic sales at store openings and or closings. Midnight madness brings the devil out in some shoppers and they behave like they are on a feeding frenzy.

Second:
Make a list of what it is you want to buy. It doesn't matter if it's for groceries or for gifts such as birthdays and Christmas. It doesn't matter if it is for a new wardrobe for work or clothing for the children. What matters is that you list what it is you want to buy, before you go shopping.

Third:

After you have prepared the above list write beside the items listed the amount you have budgeted to pay for each item and the total budgeted amount for all items.

When shopping for groceries you don't need to itemize the budgeted amount for each item but you do need to have a total budget that you must adhere to. A simple trip to the grocery store will end with disastrous consequences if you go shopping without a budget.

When you get home review what you have bought and if you discover you have purchased more than you should have and you exceeded your budget, return some items.

Except for groceries, most retailer have a policy whereby for a certain period of time and before the items are used you can return the item to the store for a full refund. Make sure you know a retailers policy before you spend your money in their store.

CHAPTER 9

❖

Credit Cards

Debt

"There are two times when you should not finance your purchases on a credit card. The first is when you can't afford it and the second time, is when you can afford it"

The above does not mean you should not use credit cards, it means, you should not finance your purchases with the card. Credit cards are beneficial when used properly and I will discuss a few benefits in a moment but first let me say that never, never miss a payment. If you must, borrow the money by getting a cash advance on another card or borrow from a friend or your employer; but never miss that minimum payment.

Why is this so important?

Because any missed payments and the number of days it took to get their payment will be reported to the credit bureau. Some card companies will increase the amount of interest they charge you, because they will consider you to be a higher risk.

Negative remarks on your credit record lower your credit score, and a lower score will result in you either being declined for credit at some future date or the credit will be rated, which means you will pay more in interest charges on any future loans.

"Never, Never, Never, Miss A Payment"

What are the benefits to you when you use credit cards to your advantage?

1) You get to keep your money, in your bank account, earning interest, for an extra period of time.
2) Many credit cards offer reward points, which can be used for travel or merchandise.
3) It allows you to make purchases when the merchandise is on sale. Whatever it is you want; if you have saved the money and it is on sale, buy it while it is on sale but make sure you pay for it when due.
4) Some cards offer extended warranties on top a manufacturer's warranty.

A few credit card companies give a grace period, which means no interest charges, for up to 25-days after the billing date, as long as the amount outstanding on the statement is paid in full by the due date shown on the statement. If your card does not have at least a 21-day grace period, get rid of it and find a card that does.

How Your Payment Gets Applied To The Balance Owing On Your Account

If you carry a balance on your credit card, the card company will apply any payments you make to your account as outlined below:

1. Insurance premiums related to your account.
2. Interest charges billed to your account.
3. Past due amount as shown on your account statement.
4. Service fees and other charges.
5. Billed purchase on which interest is payable (including any payment under an optional program):
6. Billed purchases on which interest is not yet payable; and then
7. Unbilled purchases.

Retail Store Interest

Department store interest charges are absolutely brutal, with some stores charging as much as 28%. Take a moment to review the following example. Look how much your payment would need to be each month in order to pay the balance off in 2-years and 8-years. Also compare the difference when an 18-½% and a 28% interest rate are used.

Visit www.bankrate.ca, or www.cardweb.com, as both sites have plenty of information on all the different types of credit cards, including an online calculator, where you can calculate not only the cost of credit card debt; but other debt such as car loans or mortgage debt.

Interest Rate	Outstanding Balance	Monthly Payment	Number of months to pay the balance in full
18 1/2%	$10,000.00	$501.66	24
28.0%	10,000.00	548.88	24
18 1/2%	25,000.00	500.68	96
28.0%	25,000.00	654.87	96

Credit cards should only be used as a convenience or in an emergency and not as a way to finance your purchases.

Financing goods and services on your credit card seems to be the natural way but it is a never ending and very costly trap if you do not pay the balance when due.

Retail Card Promotions

Many retailers often offer a discount on purchases you are making that day. This discount can be 10% or more, but only if you sign up then and there and charge the purchases you have made to their card.

Here is how it works.

Let's say you purchased $500.00 worth of electronics, you're ready to pay for the items and the store clerk says to you, "we are offering a 10% discount on all the purchases that you make today, if you'll just sign up for our in-store credit card."

"It's fast, convenient and will only take a minute or two." You might be thinking wow; I will save $50.00 on my purchases if I get this card. Great! I'll buy that gold USB cable for $50.00 and it will be like, getting it for free. But wait, what will you do when it's time to pay the bill?

If you're like most people you will pay the minimum balance due and the retailer will love you for it,

Why?

Because they prefer it when you don't pay the balance in full. They stand to earn a great deal more money from the interest they charge you, and the longer you take to pay the balance the more they earn. If the store interest rate is 26% and you only pay a minimum amount of 2% of the total balance outstanding; it will take you almost 6-years to pay the balance in full.

There is an opportunity here to save 10% off the purchase price but unless you are absolutely certain that you will pay the bill in full, before the due date, then just say "no thank you."

Don't set yourself up to fail. Remember you won't save any money unless you avoid those interest charges.

Penalty Charges and late payment fees

Interest is not the only area where credit card companies make money. They make money on penalty charges for late or missed payments. They will charge you some of or all of the following:

- Fees if you do not use your card for 6-months
- A fee for not carrying a balance on your account
- Transaction fees each time you use your card
- Over your credit limit fees
- Annual membership fee
- Fee for closing your account

Many card companies offer balance protection insurance and if you elect to have the balance protection insurance, they earn money on that as well.

What is balance protection insurance?

It is insurance that pays the balance owing on your credit card, if you should die or become disabled and unable to work. The card company would make the minimum payment on your behalf, but only after you have been disabled for a period of time, usually 6-months.

Only the charges already on the card, at the time of disability, are covered. If you should become disabled, any new charges after the disability are not covered.

If the disability becomes permanent, then most policies will pay the balance owing at the time of the disability, in full (read the fine print). The coverage is great; but the cost of this coverage is high. For example if you have an outstanding balance of $2,000.00 the cost for the coverage with some credit card companies can be as high as $14.80 per month.

I recommend that you speak to an insurance advisor or insurance broker about disability insurance.

Why?

Because depending on your age, health, occupation and hobbies you may be able to buy a lot more life and disability insurance for $14.80 per month than the credit card company offers.

Paying Your Credit Card Debt

If you do have credit card debt, chances are it took you a long time to get in deep, so don't expect a quick fix. Set up a plan of action to pay off the debt as soon as you can.

Make it a goal to have a certain amount of money paid off in a fixed period of time and make a life change to the way you handle debt. This is not a fad, it works and after a short while it works with very little effort.

1)   Stop buying merchandise or services on credit cards:
How will you do this? Well, the best way is to cut up all but one card. Cutting up the cards is just the first step; you must notify the issuing company that you want the cards cancelled.

Why cancel the card?

Well, the card is listed with the credit bureau and so is the amount of credit limit you have on the card. The more cards you have the more cards that are listed with the bureau and this leads to a greater possibility that your credit rating may be lowered.

Why?

Lenders don't just look at what you presently owe, they also look at and consider the potential debt you could incur and this makes you a higher credit risk. It could also hurt your chances of getting credit in the future, for other items such as automobile, boat, renovation, mortgage etc.

Cancel the card in writing as it will show credit rating bureaus that you are the one who is canceling the card and not the card company. The credit card company should notify the bureau for you.

If you do not receive confirmation that they have notified the bureau within 3 weeks then contact them to find out why. Don't treat any of these steps lightly. Closing a credit card is easy; simply send a letter with your name, address and account number to the credit card company, asking them to close the account. (See sample letter in appendix)

Be prepared for resistance from the credit card company as they will not want to lose you as an interest-paying customer. If there is a balance owing on the card they most likely will not cancel the card until they are paid in full, but this does not stop you from cutting up the card now and notifying them, as soon as you have paid the balance in full.

2) Keep The Card With The Lowest Interest Rate:

The card you keep should be the card with the lowest interest rate. If you lack discipline and you have a credit limit higher than $1,500.00 talk to the Credit Card Company and request to have your credit limit lowered to $1,500.00 or less.

Why do I recommend that you keep one card when most advisors will tell you to get rid of them all? Well financial planning is not only about saving money, it is also about being prepared for future emergencies. You never know when your car may break down, or your away from home and an accident or illness happens and you need emergency medical care or shelter.

3) Credit Card Debt Is Expensive Debt:

This is likely your most expensive debt. By expensive I mean it is costing you the most in interest. Find out how much interest you are paying on every card you have. Start with the highest interest charge. If you're like most people the credit card agreement you signed and received when you first received your card is long gone.

Look at your monthly statement. Most statements don't show the interest rate; but instead refer you back to the original agreement you signed and they reference any amendments they issued since you signed up for the card.

Contact your credit Card Company, and ask them exactly what your outstanding balance is on your account (*give them your account number*), also ask what is the effective rate of interest you are being charged.

Don't accept just any answer; you want to know the actual rate they are charging you. By law, the issuing credit Card Company must answer you truthfully.

Ask For A Lower Interest Rate

Once you know the rate, ask the person you are speaking to if they have the authority to make the decision to lower your rate. If they don't, then don't waste your time or theirs, request to speak with the person who does have the authority to lower the rate.

Once you have the decision maker on the line, ask for your rate to be lowered, tell them. "I'm calling about my account." "I have been a customer for (*the time you have been a customer*) and I have an offer for a credit card, from another card company and their interest rate is lower than rate than you are charging me."

"Will you lower my interest rate?"

Now this where you need to wait for their answer.

Wait 10-seconds.

Don't speak until they answer you. After they answer and assuming the answer will be yes ask the following questions.

What is the new rate?

When will the new rate take effect?

Don't be nervous because the absolute worse thing that can happen is they will say no to a lower rate but you are no worse off than you were before you telephoned them.

Use diplomacy, explain again if necessary, but in a non threatening manner, that you have enjoyed your business relationship with them and that you would like to continue the relationship, but unless you get a lower rate you will have no choice but to switch.

Tip: Check out what your present credit card company's competitor's rates are and have a competitor lined up in the event you need to switch.

The person you are speaking with will probably respond with something like, "You are a great customer and we really appreciate your business but the rate our competitor is quoting is an introductory rate…you'll end up paying much more when the introductory period ends."

If you found a card company with a lower rate then tell them "the rate will still be lower than what you are charging me."

Again ask "Will you lower my rate?"

If they still say no, then thank them and make the necessary arrangements with the new card Company to make the switch.

If they do agree to lower the rate, make sure you ask for their name and ID number and record this information along with the date and time you spoke to them on your statement for future reference in case you receive your next statement with no rate change reflected. If this happens you can call and speak with a Supervisor to get the problem resolved with minimal effort.

Introductory Rates For New Card Holders

There are a number of credit card companies that will offer you up to 9-months at a super low introductory rate of 1.99%. These companies are so hungry to get your business that they will do all the work for you. They notify your present credit card company that you are transferring your account to them and then they pay the balance of the account in full to them.

Sounds great!

It is great, if you use it to your advantage. All that is necessary is that you have a good credit rating. Remember that most introductory rates are good for 6-months, with a few offering 9-months, after which, the rate increases, sometimes to as high as18.99%. The rate is calculated daily on your balance and charged monthly to the account. So be sure to compare this new package with the offering your present company is willing to give you.

The issuing card company must, on the statement of conditions, or in the disclosure box, spell out everything you need to know about the term, rates, minimum payment and any and all charges that they can hit you with.

You most likely will need to get out the magnifying glass to read what it is they are telling you, because what they are telling you, are the things that if they could avoid telling you, they would avoid telling you.

The disclosure statement will also spell out what will happen if you fail to pay at least the minimum amount due by the payment date as indicated on your monthly billing statement. It may say something to the effect that, If you fail to pay on time within any six (6) month period (such as being an "Occurrence") the annual interest rate for all transactions, including those at reduced or promotional rates, could increase to as high as 24.00%, as soon as the first day of the billing cycle following the due date.

Convenience Cheques

I am sure that at one time you have received convenience cheques from your credit card company and oftentimes they offer a low introductory rate for their use. However, when this period is over, look out because the rate is usually much higher.

Once the introductory period is over the interest rate charged on cash advances or convenient cheques may actually be higher than the rate you are charged on your purchases (read the fine print). There is no grace period on cheques or cash advances. Interest charges start on the date of the cash withdrawal or the date the issuing company pays whoever is cashing the cheque.

Also, some card companies charge a minimum usage fee of $5.00 up to $10.00 just for the privilege of using the cheques or a cash withdrawal on the card.

If you get these cheques in the mail tear them up! Make you sure you tear them up, as it will help prevent identity theft. Owning a paper shredder would be a preferable and beneficial way to destroy personal mail, convenience cheques and papers that may provide private information that is hunted by identity thieves.

Contact the issuing company and tell them not to send any more cheques because if they were to end up in the wrong mailbox they could be used fraudulently and the burden of proof that you did not use them will fall on your shoulders.

After You Cut Up The Credit Card

Just cutting up the card does not make the balance disappear. Oh how we wish! Now you need to make a listing of all your credit cards. Start the list with the credit card company that charges the highest interest rate. Then show the next and the next and so on. Once the list is complete then we need to work on the payment schedule. (*See appendix for sample form*).

You must be realistic in your goal to pay off your credit card debt. It won't happen over night but with a plan of action, you will be out of debt sooner than you think.

Credit card companies would prefer it if you would pay as little as possible each month.

In fact over the last few years' credit card companies have quietly lowered the typical minimum payment amount from 5% to 2% of the balance or $10.00 whichever is higher.

Why?

They want you to believe that they are helping you; but in fact it is helping them earn more. Good for them but bad for you. If you pay $40.00 per month, which is just 2% per month on a $2,000.00 balance at 18.5% interest, it will take 8 years to pay off the balance and your interest cost will add up to more than $4,000.00 on $2,000.00 worth of purchases.

"Spend Less Than You Earn"

Control Your Spending:
If you need help to control your spending and get out of debt, there are many good credit card counseling agencies, some of which are non-profit and they can help you. But you must first recognize that you have a problem and need help. Once you recognize this, seek out a good agency.

Credit Agencies:
Avoid Any Credit Agency Who:

1) Charges high up front fees to enroll.
2) Will not send you information about their services they provide without your personal information, like credit card numbers and bank account numbers.

3) Attempts to enroll you without reviewing your personal situation. If they don't review your situation, then how are they going to make recommendations on the best place to start?
4) Does not have the qualifications and money management experience.
5) Pressures you to make voluntary contributions.

CHAPTER 10

❖

Borrowing Money

Sources of Funds

Banks are still the number one source in North America for mortgage loans but thank goodness they are not the only source as competition has forced the banks to be much more flexible with their rates and terms.

In today's market with the rates posted in the newspapers and with the use of computers, you are better able to compare mortgage rates. Most consumers realize that the "posted" or "published rate" is for those who either do not negotiate a better rate or their credit score is less than excellent.

The main sources for mortgage loans available for residential property are as follows:

- Banks
- Governments
- Seller
- Assuming an existing mortgage
- Family, friends and business associate
- Mortgage companies
- Real estate companies
- Mortgage brokers
- Lawyers

With the Internet you can do most of your research from your computer or if you prefer you can apply for the loan online. Regardless of your preference at least do the preliminary work of getting the best rates and terms etc.

If you do not have a access to a computer use the newspapers for comparative rates and then telephone prospective lenders. Get an appointment and visit the lender(s) in person. Another possibility is to find a good broker and use them.

Banks in general advertise and show a posted rate of interest that is usually higher than the interest rate charged by other lenders. However, many banks will negotiate and they do want, and need your business.

Banks like to get your other business like checking or savings accounts. Under law they cannot insist on this other business as a condition of the loan, but there is nothing preventing you from bargaining for a lower interest rate.

Before approaching the bank of your choice do your homework and get competitive rates from alternative lenders. As I mentioned earlier, banks are the major source of mortgage loans in this country but there are many other excellent sources. A good mortgage broker can place your mortgage with other lenders such as credit unions, insurance companies or private lenders. In most cases the broker is paid a finders fee by the lender but a few brokers will also charge a fee and this fee could be as much as $1,000.00.

How Much Money Can You Borrow?

All the major banks have an on line mortgage calculator to help you determine how much money you will be allowed to borrow, the amount of your payment and how much interest you will be paying over the term of the loan. Don't forget to factor in the property taxes and homeowner's insurance premium.

They also have a calculator that will let you enter your present rental payment and the calculator will tell how much of a mortgage you can get for the same payment as rent. The best calculator in my opinion is the one they have where you can enter the amount of loan you require, the interest rate you will be charged for the term you have selected and the number of years in the amortized period of the loan.

How Much Debt Can You Safely Afford?

How much debt can you afford?

Typically lenders use the Gross Debt Service Ratio (GDSR) and the Total Debt Service Ratio (TDSR).

Total Debt Service Ratio

This debt ratio should be less than 40% of your gross family income. Gross family income is defined as the total income of the borrowers to the mortgage. The lender will look at the total amount of your debt; this includes the mortgage you will have, the property taxes and any car payments, credit card payments, membership fees, heat, hydro, and tuition for the children, travel, entertainment etc. The lower you keep your TDSR the more comfortable your lender will be and the more comfortable your lifestyle will be.

Gross Debt Service Ratio

This ratio is also used to calculate the amount of payment you can afford to make for the mortgage principal, interest, property taxes and heat. All of these expenses added together should not exceed 32% of your gross family income.

There is some flexibility in this percentage because if you have little or no other debt, most lenders will allow the ratio to go higher, as high as 36% and some lenders will also take into consideration any rental income that you will receive from renting a room, a basement or a flat. In other words there is flexibility with a few lenders, which is why it is best to shop around for the right lender.

Debt Load

Just because you qualify for the mortgage doesn't mean you can afford it! Don't take on more debt than you can comfortably handle. Ratios are a great guide but you need to consider how many children you have and what it will cost you to raise them to adulthood. Also take into consideration you and your partner's lifestyle in general.

Do you eat in restaurants often and or take luxury vacations every year? Do you buy expensive clothes or luxury items? Do you have expensive memberships in various clubs or fitness centers?

If this is the lifestyle you enjoy, and you have no intention of stopping or cutting back on expenses, then be sure to consider these expenses as part of your monthly costs when you borrow money.

You need to consider all your present expenses when taking on a mortgage. If you over extend yourself financially, the stress of trying to make your payments will quickly negate the satisfaction of home ownership and may result in you losing everything you have worked so hard to achieve.

Life Insurance

Lenders' may offer you a life insurance policy on the mortgage. The purpose of which would be to pay off the mortgage, in the event of your death?

Check the policy that they are offering, because most policies reduce the value of the insurance as you pay down the principal amount owing on the mortgage, but in most cases the premium remains the same.

The lender cannot insist that you take their insurance. I do however, recommend that you speak to a life insurance agent or broker about a life insurance policy. Compare their policy with the lenders policy, as you most likely will find the insurance company to be cheaper.

By purchasing a life insurance policy for a term that is as long as the mortgage term from your insurance agent or broker, your beneficiary would receive the benefit amount of the policy.

This benefit would be paid regardless of the amount that is left owing on the mortgage. If your health were to change for the worse, during the term and you were unable to get insurance or a policy you could afford at the time of the health change, at least you would still have this term policy.

If you and your partner's income were used to pay the mortgage then it would be a good idea to have insurance on each of you. If the death benefit of the policy is for $200,000.00 and you die during the policy term, your estate would be paid the full $200,000.00.

Interest you will pay

In Canada, the interest you pay on a mortgage is in most cases calculated semiannually and not in advance. Simply said "An interest rate of 5.25% calculated semiannually is actually costing you an effective interest rate of 5.3077% annually." The lender must advise you in writing, of any fees you will be charged for setting up the mortgage, and this includes the interest rate, the effective interest rate and how much the interest will cost you, in dollars and cents, over the term of the mortgage you have selected.

American mortgage or deed of trust interest is usually calculated monthly and not in advance. However, the more times interest is calculated the higher the effective rate of interest is to the borrower. So when using amortization tables or an online mortgage calculator, be sure to use to use the one that applies to your country.

Don't assume that all lenders calculate their interest semi-annually, (Canada) or monthly (U.S.A). Most will, but it is important for you to realize that the interest rate that you are quoted is the rate of interest that you will be charged; but it does not tell the complete story, because it is the effective rate of interest that is used to calculate your total interest cost. The more frequently the interest rate is calculated, the higher the cost.

The statement "not in advance" simply means, you make your first mortgage payment at the end of the payment period you selected. If you pay your mortgage monthly, then at the end of the month you will have had the use of the money for that month and now you make your payment.

"Spend Less Than You Earn"

CHAPTER 11

❖

Debt Consolidation

If you're not too far in debt and have a good credit rating you may be able to negotiate with a credit card company to have your debt consolidated on one card. Again, look for the lowest interest rate. When they quote you a rate ask them "Is that the best you can do?"

Pause and wait for their answer. Remember the 10-second rule.

Also ask what the introductory rate is!

Remember credit card debt is your most expensive debt and if circumstances permit, use your line of credit, or place a second mortgage on your property.

Why?

Because the interest cost would be much lower for this type of debt. Regardless of how you consolidate your debt you need to start work on getting out of debt completely. If you are presently paying for a mortgage on your own home, there are companies out there that will offer to consolidate your credit card debt with your mortgage debt so that you end up with one easy payment.

You must!

Use caution when considering this option as some use different amortization periods in their example to make their offer look better than what you are presently paying.

I recently received an offer in the mail to consolidate credit card debt with mortgage debt. The example showed how much $25,000.00 of credit card debt and how much a $200,000.00 mortgage would be on a monthly basis. The mortgage payment would be $1,309.48 per month, if the interest rate was fixed at 6.25% interest and the monthly payment on $25,000.00 of credit card debt at 18.50% interest is $850.00, making a total payment of $2,059.48.

They went on to show, if you were to consolidate the credit card debt and mortgage debt with them, their loan of $225,000.00, would be loaned to you at a variable interest rate of 5.65% interest. (*see mortgage section on interest rates for details on variable vs. fixed term*). Your new monthly payment would go down to $1,173.47; this means your new monthly payment will save you $886.01. Trust me when I say this monthly payment savings will actually cost you plenty both in interest expense and extra time in years to pay off the mortgage. How is it they can lower the payment amount on a loan that is $25,000.00 higher?

It's possible because they are not telling you the full story.

1) The amortization period on the $200,000.00 of debt is 25 years. (*Not shown in example*)
2) The amortization period on the $225,000.00 of debt is 40 years. (*Shown in the example but in very small print*)
3) In the United States of America you can renegotiate your mortgage at any time and most banks will not charge a penalty for closing out the old mortgage. They may charge administrative fees but not a penalty. Check the cost of these fees before you agree to anything.

In Canada a company offering you a new mortgage, is not obliged to tell you that if your old mortgage is not up for renewal, it may cost you either 3 months penalty interest or an interest rate differential (IRD) (*See chapter 21 for the further details*) This penalty interest is in addition to legal and other fees, in order to discharge your $200,000.00 mortgage. This penalty could cost you more than $5,000.00.

4) The interest you will pay on your present 25-year $200,000.00 mortgage is $192,846.40 if the interest remained constant at the 6.25%. However, by switching to the 40 year, $225,000.00 mortgage you will pay $338,257.45, which is $145,411.05 more than staying with your 25-year mortgage? Plus you will be in debt 15 years longer.

Be careful when comparing companies and their monthly payment because the monthly payment does not give you all the information you need to make the right decision.

CHAPTER 12

❖

How To Save As Much Money As Possible On Your Purchases

T his is a fun chapter where you will learn the art of negotiating for the best table in a restaurant, a lower interest rate, and how to get a better price on almost everything you buy.

"The Mind Doesn't Listen Until The Heart Gives Its Permission"

Did you know that just about everyone makes the buying decision with their heart (emotion) and then they justify it, in their mind? (logic)

The focus of this book is to teach you how to get out of debt, save money on those items you do buy and not spend any more than absolutely necessary.

If you have more money than you know what to do with, then skip this chapter and read the rest of the book.

ABM

Let's start this chapter by discussing withdrawal fees when you use an ABM machine as this is an area where you can begin saving money with almost no effort. Did you know that by withdrawing cash from any ABM machine other than your own banks machine will cost you money?

A bank other than your own will typically charge you $1.50 per withdrawal plus in some cases a service of an additional $.50 per transaction. Use one of these machines once a week and your spending $96.00 a year in fees you need not pay.

If you use the machine in places other than banks such as stores, casinos, airports etc. you will pay even more.

Debit Cards

Many more convenience stores are starting to charge you a fee for using a debit card for purchases of less than $3.00.

Why?

Because they are charged a fee on all transactions they place on their account and in some cases they are charged $.50 per transaction. This could result in the store losing money as the profit on a $1.00 item would not be enough to cover the charge the store would pay.

They should post a sign stating that they will add a small amount to your purchase if it is for less than $3.00 but many don't. Watch what you are paying to be sure this charge is not being added to your bill.

Also, many banks also charge a transaction fee when you use as "debit" and key in a pin number. If you use the card as a "credit" and sign for the purchase you can avoid the transaction fee.

Furniture And Appliances

I learned a long time ago that just about everything is negotiable, especially the price. The way to look at this is, if you ask for a better price and are told no, you are no worse off than before you asked.

Why?

Because you are in same position as you were before you asked, no worse you just didn't get a better price. What is there to lose by asking for a better price?

Nothing!

There is no need to wait for a sale if you just learn to ask for a better price and this includes asking for a lower interest rate when you borrow money. The following techniques will teach you how to negotiate a better deal.

The one thing I recommend that you never do is never negotiate for something unless you have decided that you want that item or service; don't waste your time on something you have little or no interest in. What does it matter how much it will cost if it's not what you want.

OK, so now you've decided on the new couch for the living room, or that dining room table that you have been saving for, over the last year. So what do you do now?

Most people look at the price and say "that's not bad", even when it is. You may say "that's more than we want to spend" at which point the salesperson will usually attempt to win you over by making offers for an easy payment plan.

How?

By offering you a special financing deal with no payments for a year, or more.

If you have saved the money and you're planning to pay with cash, then you don't care about the extended financing plan that is being offered. When offered such a plan, tell them your going to pay cash if the price is good.

There was a time that if you bought something with cash, the retailer would automatically give you a big discount. They rarely do that now because they earn more money when you charge it to their retail card and pay it over time. But it never hurts to ask.

Pay No Interest

I'm sure you have seen the specials where you can buy something now and not make any payments for one, two, and three years. In most cases the retailer sells this financing arrangement to a finance company because the cost to them is low; they get their money from the finance company within 30-days and they distance themselves from the financing altogether.

I must caution you however to read the fine print, you know the print, where you need to use a magnifying glass, in order to be able to see it.

Why?

Let's say the date that the merchandise must be paid in full is 2-years from today's date and let's say you have decided not to make any payments until that date. Make sure you pay it in full on or before this date because many of these agreements state that you must pay the complete balance outstanding in full by midnight of that due date otherwise they will charge interest back to the date of when you purchased the goods.

Now that could be a nasty surprise, because you now owe a lot more money than you expected and those monthly payments will start and continue until the term of the agreement is over and the full amount owing has been paid.

Let me say it again, the problem is because you did not pay the amount owing in full by the due date, you now owe the original amount, plus interest, and the interest is calculated back to the date of purchase. You now owe back interest plus current interest for as long as it takes you to pay the amount back. Be sure to read the fine print.

A little technique you can use to your advantage is, when you purchase anything under an agreement such as this, is to take the total amount owing and divide it by the number of months until the date of the final payment is due. Start repaying it now and continue to make monthly payments each and every month until paid in full.

By doing it this way you will avoid having to pay any interest charges because you will have paid the full amount owing before the due date, but remember, do not be a day late.

The nice thing about using the above technique, is if you already have the money saved you get to keep it in a high interest savings account while you pay off part of the purchase, interest free, every month. Only do this if you have a lot of discipline, if not then use the cash!

Don't discuss financing until after you have negotiated the best possible price, as they are two different things. Once you are told a price that you like, accept it and continue negotiating. Negotiate for free delivery, extra warranty or financing if you really need to finance what it is you are buying.

It is best, if you could hold off buying until you have the cash. If you can't wait to buy, and you feel that this price is the best you can get or it is a one of a kind item and you are afraid you will never be able to get it again at the price they are offering then negotiate the interest charge and other payment terms.

If you don't like the price or finance charges, walk away from the offer. I have walked away, only to have the salesperson come out to the parking lot with a better offer.

Let's take a look at the worst scenario, you walk and they don't make a better offer.

So what!

If you really want the item, go back an hour later or the next day or on the weekend and ask if they are now willing to negotiate, if they say no and the price offered is the best they can do, decide, if you want to pay their price. If you do, then buy it. If not, walk away again and go to another store and buy from someone who is willing to negotiate.

One last point though, when you ask someone for a better price, or better terms, wait for the answer, and don't speak too soon. 10-seconds of silence will seem like an eternity but it is only 10-seconds. They will answer and most likely before the 10-second mark.

I can't say it enough.

Wait 10-seconds.

While you are waiting look them in the eye and smile. Never ask a question with an answer. Such as "I guess this is your best price." Ask instead "Is this your best price?"

Hotels & Their Rates

As you know hotels offer many different rates, they offer a corporate rate, a frequent guest rate, a senior's rate, a rate for booking online and a weekend or holiday rate.

Regardless of the rate they offer, always ask "Is that the best rate you have?" or "can you do better?'

Again, let me remind you, you will be no worse off than you would have been, if you hadn't asked, but one thing is for sure, if you don't ask, the answer is already no.

If they do say no to a further discount, then ask if you can have an upgraded room for the price they are asking.

If they still say no, then call another hotel in the area where you want to stay and check out their rates.

It doesn't cost you anything to negotiate. If you need a late check out time, negotiate it, in advance. Most hotels are flexible on check out times because they can't clean all the rooms at the same time. If you ask they will usually schedule your room near the end of the cycle.

Restaurant Reservations

How many times have you made a reservation at a restaurant and they wanted to sit you by the kitchen, the outside door, or in the center of the restaurant where you have almost no privacy?

Try this the next time you make a reservation at a restaurant. Say to them, using these words "we are celebrating and would like it if you would be so kind as to give us your best table."

You don't have to tell them what you are celebrating it may be you're celebrating the fact that you're still alive or it's your birthday, or an anniversary, promotion etc.

These hot words "**we are celebrating**" will usually get you one of the best seats in the restaurant.

Buying Clothes

New:

It pays to shop around for all purchases, including clothing. I buy top of the line clothing and I seldom pay regular price. What I do is I wait, for a sale.

A sale always comes and when it does, I will buy $100.00 shirts for $35.00 to $40.00 each. I buy shoes, slacks, jeans and suits the same way. The secret is to have your money saved so that when there is a sale you can buy more than one of the items you are after. I will often buy 5 or 6 shirts at the same time and or 2 to 3 pairs of shoes. It not only saves me money but it saves a lot of time.

Used Clothes:

In tough economic times it may be necessary to shop at a store that sells used items. Don't be too quick to criticize buying merchandise at these stores as most of what they sell is of excellent quality. It is also a great place to buy your kids toys or games. Young kids don't care and in many cases they can't tell the difference.

Pawn Shops:

Most people don't think about going to a pawnshop to buy electronic items, jewelry, watches, toasters, games, toys etc. They should however, because the shop only takes items that are in great shape. Remember people who in many cases have fallen on hard times and need some emergency cash sell these items to the shop. I don't know a major city that does not have at least one pawnshop. Check on line or in your telephone book for a location nearest you.

Buying Clubs (Wholesale)

Not all buying clubs are the same, some are great and others are questionable. Let me explain. Recently my wife Susan and I went to a buying club. I won't name them but you most likely have seen their advertisements on television.

In their advertisements they show customers giving testimonials on how much money they saved by buying new kitchen cabinets, countertops and furniture etc., from the buying club instead of the retailer.

My wife saw one of these advertisements on television and telephoned the club to get more information, they were very pleasant, helpful and accommodating. They mailed her a very nice colour brochure and followed up with a telephone call, to set up an appointment for her and I to visit them.

An appointment was arranged and off we went on Saturday for our scheduled appointment time of 10:00am. We met a very nice young lady whose job it was to escort us to the main sitting area.

Once there we sat at a table, which allowed us reasonable privacy so she could have an informal chat with us about why we were there and what it was we were looking to buy at that time. She also asked where we lived and how long we lived there etc. She was doing her best to get us to relax and at the same time learn a lot more about us.

After about 10-minutes of informal chitchat we were introduced to the manager and escorted into another room where they had chairs set up facing a large television. The manager told us the presentation would start shortly and it did.

He started the presentation by explaining how long the buying club had been in business and how the club was able to buy direct from the manufacturer, just as retailers were.

He went on to explain, all the retailers were ripping us off.

How were the retailers ripping us off?

They were ripping us off by charging us much more than the buying club would for the same items sold by the retailer.

After listening to him for about 6 or 7 minutes he turned the television on and played a prerecorded message about the benefits of belonging to their club. The recording showed more testimonials from customers about how much money they saved, it went on to explain a few more details about the benefits of club membership and their buying power.

The manager returned and showed examples of advertisements from retailers who ran sale ads on various products such as leather sofas, LCD and plasma television sets, hardwood flooring etc.

The manager was making a case for membership in their club. He was giving us examples of the retail price and the price to buy directly from the club. The average savings was approximately 25%.

Finally he got to the part I like. The manager explained how much it was going to cost to be a member of their club.

I hope you're sitting down while reading this because the cost was much more than I would have thought and I don't want you to fall over.

How much?

Plenty!

In Toronto, Canada the cost to be a member of their club for the first 10-years was $6,510.00. The first 3-years would cost $4,680.00 and the next 7-years would cost $261.00 per year. He also said "the average cost per year for 10-years would be $651.00 per year."

However, the club wanted the $4,680.00 that day, and they were quick to tell us that this could be financed over a 3-year period.

At this point, my wife and I, along with about 20 others, were led back into the main office to see their catalogues while he explained in more detail how the system would work and just how easy it would be to select whatever it was you wanted to order from a catalogue, for your home or office.

Each page in the catalogue gave the suggested retail price and the price the club, would charge. It was a good presentation; however, they failed to keep their cost comparisons up to date.

Why?

Because a couple of the retail price examples they gave us, were out of date, in fact, the retail sale price they showed was more than what the retailer's regular price is now! In other words they showed us out of date advertisements.

Regardless whether a price was out of date or not, the average saving of 25% does not justify being a member.

To summarize, if you paid the membership fee in full, without financing and if on average you were able to save 25% of the cost on the items you bought by buying from the club you would need to purchase $26,028.00 of merchandise, just to break even.

If you financed the $4,680.00 that you were required to give them that day, over 3-years and added the finance charges to the $4,680.00 you would need to buy at least $37,250.00 of merchandise just to break even.

Think about what I just said, after you pay the club, $4,680.00 plus interest charges you will need to buy $37,250.00 in merchandise, just to get back an amount equal to the money you gave them.

Once you spent the $37,250.00 in merchandise anything you bought after that would actually save you money.

I am not saying that buying club memberships are a waste of money; but I am saying that this is a lot of money for a membership so beware of the cost versus the benefits you will receive.

Ask yourself this question.

Will I spend more on merchandise for my home than the breakeven amount that I need to spend in order to start saving money over the 10-year period? If your answer is yes then joining the club may very well work out to be a good deal for you. I do hope it works for you!

Do not overlook what I said earlier, "we buy with the heart (emotion) and we justify the purchase with our mind (logic)."

What does this mean?

It means when you buy something such as a product or service, you buy it for many different reasons. You buy because you like it. You buy because you want it. You buy because you need it. You buy because a family member needs or wants it; but you never buy anything, just to save money. You want to save money when you do buy but buying to save money is not the way to do it.

If you're like most of us, I am sure you get great pleasure in having something new and when you make a major and sometimes a minor purchase, is it not more fun and pleasurable to shop in person with a friend or love one?

You go to the retailer to see, touch, try it on, check out the size, and compare styles and materials to match with your drapes, wall and floor coverings and of course to do a little comparative shopping?

Most retailers will accept returns at no cost to you even after you have used them for a short period of time. Will the buying club do this? Make sure they will!

I'll leave this topic on one last point. Retail buyers for the largest retailers in the world only buy from a manufacturer's catalogue after they have first seen and in many cases tested the product.

Lease vs. Buying An Automobile

I am often asked whether it is better to lease or to buy an automobile. The short answer is "It depends". Depends on what? Well it depends on whether you are the type of person who wants to drive a new vehicle every 2 or 3 years or the type of person who would prefer to purchase the automobile and drive it for 7 to 10-years. In most cases if you drive the car for 10-years you will be payment free after 5-years and the cost of ownership will be a lot less than leasing.

If you want a new vehicle every 2 to 3-years then leasing is probably a good option for you, especially if you lease a vehicle that depreciates at a faster rate than average.

Many businesses prefer to lease their vehicles for many reasons including tax benefits that you as an individual do not get unless the car is used for business purposes. They also like to control their costs and by leasing they know what it will cost them to lease the car over the lease period (no depreciation surprises) and for the most part they want their sales representatives driving newer cars as they usually require fewer repairs and give companies a better corporate image.

One last caveat when leasing a vehicle, make sure you know the allowable mileage that you may drive the vehicle during the period of the lease without incurring any additional penalty charges. If you believe you will drive more than the allotted miles during the term of the lease, calculate what the charge will be to you for the extra mileage.

If the cost for each additional mile (kilometer) you drive over and above the allowable limit adds thousands of dollars to the cost of the lease then it would probably be best if you bought the vehicle and sold it at the end of 3-years of driving.

If the model of vehicle you drive has a history then you can with reasonable certainty, estimate its depreciation rate over the first 3 to 4-years of the auto's life. Remember this though; depreciation is the highest in the first year of driving. In fact some models will depreciate as much as 50% in the first year.

As soon as you drive the car off the lot you can expect the car to depreciate at least 30% and in some cases as much as 40 to 50%.

Why is this?

Well the new car is now a used car.

Once the lease is signed, there is no easy way to end the lease. In other words if you get a vehicle you don't like, one that requires a lot of repairs or your financial circumstances change and you want to turn it back in after 21-months of driving with 15-months remaining on the lease you will be:

1) Charged a high penalty for the privilege to turn it in early or
2) You will be held responsible to pay for the 15-months remaining on the lease, whether or not you keep it.

Also keep in mind; you are responsible to maintain the leased vehicle in good condition, in fact when you return the vehicle at the end of the lease any damage beyond reasonable wear and tear is your responsibility and you will be charged accordingly.

Make sure you understand what the leasing company's definition of reasonable wear and tear is!

At the time of writing this book a couple of car manufactures no longer lease their cars or trucks. This may mean you will need a third party leasing company. One thing is for sure; the lease rate you will pay will be higher than it once was because the vehicles are depreciating much faster than the manufacturers originally estimated.

Buying A Used Automobile

OK, you have made the decision to buy your automobile.

What now?

Now you need to decide if you are motivated financially or emotionally. From a financial point of view you will be much better off if you were to buy a used car or should I say, "previously owned car." Previously owned sounds so much better, don't you agree?

Why buy a previously owned vehicle? The best reason is because you will save a lot of money. A car loses most of its value as soon as it is sold and driven from the lot. Let someone else pay for the new car smell. I suggest you buy a 5 or 6 year old, luxury car preferably with low mileage.

Luxury cars are built so well that with proper care you will have an auto that should give you a trouble free, rattle free, comfortable ride for another 6 to 8 years. Luxury car styling changes very little, so little, that most people would have no idea you're driving a 6-year-old car.

Did you know most self-made millionaires never buy a new car; they buy a 3 to 4-year old luxury car?

Vehicles' History

When buying a resale car, make sure you have it inspected by an independent mechanic for both mechanical fitness and body fitness. Have the body and frame checked to ensure you are not buying a car that has been in a major accident. Looks are important but safety is more important.

Also, if you plan on buying the vehicle from a private seller, make sure you check out the history of the car. Look for information on who presently owns the vehicle to be sure it is not stolen. Also check to find out who previously owned the vehicle and make sure there is no money owing on the vehicle.

Why?

Because you may be responsible for any outstanding monies (loan) owing on the vehicle. There are on line services that can provide this information quickly at a reasonable price.

Price Check Before Visiting The Car Dealer:

Before shopping for any vehicle do your homework. Check the advertisements for the car you have in mind. Read the newspapers and Buy and Sell magazines to get an idea on how much you will need to pay for a quality car.

This step won't take a lot of time but it may save you many thousands of dollars when it's time to negotiate the price. Beware of the deal that seems too good to be true because it usually is. Also, never buy a car from anyone who does not have a fixed address.

Negotiate

Whether you buy or lease, remember to negotiate. As discussed earlier, just about everything is negotiable including the price of the vehicle. The lease rate is calculated on the purchase price. Most people assume that if you lease the vehicle that the price is carved in stone (fixed) and that you must accept what is being offered by the dealership.

Far from it!

Negotiate! Negotiate! Negotiate!

Always ask the question "Is this your best price?" Once you have negotiated the best price; it is time to ask "What else are you offering me in order for me to make a final decision?"

Wait for the answer.

Remember the 10-second rule I gave in a previous chapter.

Ask for extra warranty, free maintenance for the first year, free floor mats, free car washes. Don't get too carried away here, make sure your requests are reasonable because all good negotiating should end up being a win win combination for both parties.

As explained earlier always be prepared to walk away from the deal. Remember, you can always go back if you can't find a better deal anywhere else.

In my experience if the deal is doable, the deal gets done. I have on more than one occasion walked away from a deal and got as far as the parking lot, when the salesperson has come running up to me and said. "You have a deal, come back inside and we will finish up the paper work."

I once went with my father to negotiate on his behalf the purchase of a new Ford Mustang. We found the perfect Mustang for him, it was silver gray and it was available immediately. My dad was exploding with enthusiasm and the sales person picked up on this. I tried to negotiate the deal but the salesman was asking for list price and he was so certain that he would get it; he would not budge on the price.

Remember what I taught you to do. Walk away. Well we did just that. We walked. I wasn't worried, as I was certain that we would get the same type of car, at another dealership for less money and if we didn't we would not be any worse off, because we could return and buy this vehicle.

We left, but before we left, I went back over to the car my dad wanted and wrote down the cars serial number.

On the way to the next dealership, which was only a few blocks from my dad's home, I reminded my dad not to show too much excitement. It is OK to show interest but refrain from excitement.

We spoke to the saleswomen about the model of car my dad was interested in. They had the model, but not in the silver gray he liked.

The saleswomen said. "I can get the model you want in the colour you want from another dealership."

How was this possible?

It was possible because dealerships trade models with each other all the time. This is called Dealer exchange or DX. That's great I said "but at what price? The price will be exactly what your looking for."

Her first offer was list price less 5%. Now we are off to a good start. We ended up agreeing to list price less 12% plus free mats and free oil changes for the first two years.

Not Bad! But wait! Remember I wrote down the serial number of the car? When my dad picked up the car at the dealership, it was not just the same make and model of car he wanted; it was the same car. The serial number of the car was the number I wrote down. So you see with positive thinking and good negotiating, everything worked out well.

CHAPTER 13

❖

Reasons to Buy Or
Not Buy A Home

Buying and eventually owning your own home (house or condominium) is the North American dream. It will give you an absolutely wonderful feeling and it will get you started on your road to financial independence. Keep in mind that this is a long-term investment, as the market will occasionally go down and if you sell in a down market you may very well lose money. For those people who were forced to sell in the USA in 2007 and 2008 the loss has been substantial. Canadian home values started falling at the end of 2008 by as much as 12%.

Six Reasons Why Buying Your Own Home Is A Great Idea

1) Pride of ownership:
    When you own your own home, you will have a sense of pride; knowing that your hard work is for many worthwhile reasons, and not just shelter. I knew a gentleman and his wife who rented the same house for 18 years. He was always afraid to buy because he had this notion that if he was unable to pay the mortgage he would lose the home and everything else he owned. Instead he rented a house for 18-years and never missed a rent payment during that time.

Based on the amount of rent he paid over those 18-years he could have bought and paid for his-own home. Finally, as his retirement years approached, his daughter convinced him to buy and he spent his final 5 years of life, living in his own home. This accomplishment filled him with pride and joy.

By the way, when he gave his notice to the landlord that he would be moving, the landlord did not even thank him for all his years as an excellent tenant nor did he say goodbye.

2) Freedom to Decorate:

If you live in your own house you can landscape the property as you desire, grow your own vegetables, or add an addition on to the house (with permission and the proper permits from the local government), or if you prefer do nothing at all. You now have a choice. If you live in your own house or condominium you can decorate the walls, floors or ceiling any way you like.

When building inside or out you will need to abide by the local by-laws, or abide by condominium rules; but for the most part you are free to make decorating changes to the inside of your home to best suit your taste and needs without the need for a permit.

3) Forced Investment Builds Equity:

Buying a home you can afford is a great way to get started on the road of financial independence. Its like forced savings. As you make your mortgage payments, the first part of the payment pays the interest and the remainder goes toward the principal. Since equity is the difference between what you owe on an asset and what the asset is worth, your net worth is going up.

Over the last 50 years there have only been a few periods of time lasting 3 to 4 years where home prices have actually declined. For most of the last 50 years home prices have increased on an average of 6%.

Keep in mind this 6% is average and in many locations where the economy is booming or in a local, where land has become scarce, the increase has been much higher.

However, it is not always wine and roses, as there are undesirable locations, such as localities where there is a lot of crime or where a large employer has been forced to close the business and relocate because of economic conditions.

You must never assume that all real estate will increase in value but for the most part and for most locations it will. At the time of writing this book, there are many areas in the USA where home prices have fallen as much as 50% with no bottom in site.

I recommend that you buy as much home as you can afford, without being mortgage poor. (See also paragraph on leverage)

Why?

The present tax structure in Canada is favorable to home ownership. The home you purchase and live in is classified as your principal residence and as it increases in value these increases are tax-free. This increased value remains tax-free, even when you sell or leave the home to your heirs.

Learn to live within your means and don't take on more debt than you can comfortably handle. If you over-extend yourself with debt, the stress of trying to make your payments will quickly negate the satisfaction of home ownership and may result in you losing everything, which you have worked so hard to achieve.

Again I must remind you, not to buy more home than you can afford to make the payments on. Also, do not borrow more money and increase your mortgage, just because the equity in the home has increased. Get the home paid for as soon as you can.

Our American friends have a cap on how much the value of their home can increase before they are required to pay tax on the capital gain. Be sure to check with a tax specialist in the respective area you are planning to buy your home.

American's are also allowed to deduct the interest they pay on their mortgage from their personal taxes. Check with a tax advisor or the Internal Revenue Service for the amount of this deduction. This deduction saves the homeowner a lot of money each year on their income taxes. However, I believe it encourages people to take on more debt because of the tax right off.

Don't increase your mortgage to save taxes, get your mortgage paid off and then you will be able to save more money for retirement.

No investment should ever be made if it is made for the sole purpose of saving taxes. Each investment must stand on its own merits, before tax and any savings derived from a good honest tax deduction is a bonus.

4) Leverage:

Leverage means that you can use a small amount of your own money and borrow the rest. How does this work? Well if you bought a $300,000.00 home and you made a down payment of $30,000.00 and a year later the home increased in value by 6%, this would amount to $18,000.00. Wow,

$18,000.00 on top of the $30,000.00 you invested, earned you a 60% return.

5) Shortage of Land:

Land is finite - there won't be any more. Population increases and a decreasing supply of serviced land are two of the main factors that affect land values. There is less available serviced land because of the high cost of installing the infrastructure to handle the increased traffic, clean drinking water, sewage, hospitals and schools.

6) Income Potential:

To earn extra money to help with the mortgage payment, you can where allowed (check with your local municipality) rent out your basement or the second floor of your home. If you need more space and feel that renting the basement or upstairs would make it too crowded for you, then rent a single room.

Make sure you check the prospective tenants' references because the last thing you want is a situation where you do not get paid or you end up with undesirable tenants. After checking with their present landlord, check with the previous landlord. (*Especially if they have only lived there for a short period of time*) the best reference will likely be from the prospective tenant's previous landlord.

Why?

Because the reference you get from the landlord where they are no longer living, will in most cases be the most reliable. If they are undesirable tenants where they presently live their landlord may give them a good reference just to get rid of them.

If you are operating a small business, and local bylaws permit you could operate the business from your home and a tax deduction may allow you to deduct a portion of your expenses from your rental or business income.

What expenses?

Expenses such as heat, hydro, and the interest cost on the mortgage may be deducted. Check with a tax accountant or the tax department, for expert advice on what you will be allowed to deduct.

Four Reasons for Not Wanting to Buy Your Own Home

1) You can't afford it:

This is probably the best reason for not wanting to buy your own home. Not only will you have a mortgage payment but you will also need to pay property taxes, homeowners insurance, utility expenses and upkeep costs. The interest rate you are initially charged may balloon in size after two to three years and you may not be able to afford to keep paying. If you know the interest rate will increase make sure that you also know with reasonable certainty that you will be able to afford it at the new rate.

2) Lack of Liquidity:

Property for the most part takes time to sell. Sometimes in a slow market it can take 6-months or more. If your home is located in the countryside then 6 to 12-months is more likely the norm. If you need to sell in a hurry you may be forced to lower the price more than you would like, just to get the home sold.

3) Holding period:

Unless you bought when the housing market was booming, you should expect to stay in your home for at least seven to 10-years. This should give you a chance to build enough equity in the home. This period will allow you time to have sufficient money to pay for your real estate expenses to sell it and buy a new home. You will also need enough money to pay your legal costs, moving costs and other fees.

On a 25-year mortgage term, you will after 5-years of mortgage payments, have only reduced the amount owing on the mortgage loan by approximately 5%. Also keep in mind that unless the sale were to close on the day the mortgage term is up, you will be expected to pay either a 3-month interest penalty or the interest rate differential whichever is greatest. (*Canada only*)

The best way to build wealth is to stay in your home as long as possible, the more you sell and buy the more it will cost you. Many millionaires and a few billionaires stay in their homes for 20 years or more.

4) Government Regulations:

Sometimes the government will expropriate and or require a right away on your property. The government must however, have a valid reason, such as a necessary road widening, a new or expanding airport, a new highway, hospital or a school. You may not like it but you can't stop progress and the government is obligated to pay a fair price.

❖

CHAPTER 14

Before You Buy

Are you ready to buy?

Great, you now know the general area where you would like to live, how much you can afford and you have been pre-approved for the mortgage.

Now to find the home of your dreams but before you sign on the dotted line I would like to remind you that buying a home is a very serious commitment, one that you will be paying for, for a very long time.

Take your time, and get the right professionals on your team.

Make sure your team members are professional, qualified and experienced. Also, make sure your chemistry matches with theirs and you have the confidence and feel comfortable working with him or her.

Be comfortable with their attitude, approach, and commitment to you. Make sure they have integrity and be sure to ask about their fees and other charges upfront before they have started working for you, this way there will be no unpleasant surprises.

Lawyer

It is essential that you obtain a lawyer who is experienced in property law to represent and protect your interests before the purchase takes place. The legal jungle is a complicated one and there are many potential legal pitfalls for the novice when buying real estate.

The "agreement for purchase and sale" and related documents are complex and you will need a lawyer, so choose your lawyer carefully!

Realtor

There are many advantages to selecting a realtor that you are comfortable with and one whom you can trust to give you the best advice as to which property will best meet your needs.

Since the sales commission is included in the selling price of the home it is ultimately you the buyer who is paying the commission to the agent.

There are a few good part time agents; but my experience has shown it is best to find an agent who works full time as a realtor, one who knows what properties are available and it's high and low points.

Find an agent that will screen the available homes to find those homes that fit your wish list. This is the list that spells out what you would like the home to have and the things that you consider the home must have as a minimum such as a garage or large lot. The list will help you to focus on your needs and wants and it will save both you and the agent time and avoid them having to drag you out, to see every available property.

The seller's agent or sub-agent can legally act for you, and they can present the seller with "the offer to purchase." However, to avoid any possible conflict I recommend you use your own agent (buyer broker) to represent you and have her present the "offer to purchase" to the seller and their agent.

Use an agent that has very effective negotiating skills and one who will be candid with you in suggesting a realistic offering price. One who will give you their reasons for why they recommend a certain strategy.

Give your agent exclusivity to work for you. If you visit an open house let the agent at the open house know another agent represents you and inform your agent of the visit.

If you become dissatisfied with your agent for any reason, find another agent as soon as possible. Hire slow and fire fast is the best way to save you money and grief.

Private Sale

I tried to sell our last home with real estate agents; actually I had tried two different real estate firms and agents.

I gave the first agent 4-months and the second agent 3-months to sell my home. To be fair, the second agent worked very hard to sell my home but the home was located in a neighborhood where they were still building new homes at a lower price than ours and with the selling commission added to the price of our home, meant it was over priced.

Since the agents were unwilling to lower their commission, and I was unwilling to lower the price any further I decided to sell the home privately. It is not difficult to sell your own home privately but it does require a lot of work and unless you know what you are doing, don't do it. Use an expert in real estate sales.

Let me tell you a little story on why it is important to work with an agent you trust. When I sold the home privately. I purchased signage and advertised in the newspapers with colour pictures of my home. I also had an open house on the weekends.

One Saturday afternoon after we had a 4-hour open house I received a telephone call from a young couple that was relocating from the United States and wanted to come over to see our home that evening.

They said "they drove by the home with their agent earlier in the day but they did not come in at the time, they wanted to come in; but their agent wasn't interested." It made sense for the agent not to want to show the house at that time, since he did not have an agreement with my wife and I; and without an agreement, he would not have been paid any commission. I can fully understand that, the problem I have is the agent told two lies. The first lie was, he said he saw the inside of our home and the second lie, was that it was a dump inside.

About a half hour after the couple's telephone call I received another call, this time it was from an agent who said "he had a couple that was in from out of town for a few days and they were interested in seeing our home." He asked, "if I would be interested in giving him the listing". My first thought was it must be the same couple but I decided to keep this information to myself. The couple was already on the way to our home so why would I want to pay a commission if I didn't need to.

The agent was asking for a commission of 6% and a 30-day listing. Since, I was asking $380,000.00 for the home it meant there would be a commission of $22,800.00. At this price I said I was not interested but I suggested a fee of $5,000.00 and a 48-hour listing. He would not lower his commission and

I would not raise my offer, especially when I was thinking it was the same couple.

The couple did come to see the home, and fell in love with it. They asked if it would be OK for them to return the next day to see it once more in the daylight.

When they returned on Sunday they wanted to buy the home and we agreed to a price of $375,000.00. They returned on Monday with a deposit cheque and the "offer to purchase" in writing from their lawyer. In parting the husband made the comment that he felt bad for the agent who drove them around to see a few homes in the neighborhood and that because they were purchasing the home directly from us their agent would not receive any sales commission.

I asked the husband the sales agents' name and when he told me I said, "your agent, did telephone on Saturday night about a ½ hour after you. I explained that I offered the real estate agent a $5,000.00 sales commission and a 48-hour listing if the home sold. Once the husband realized that the agent could have made an easy $5,000.00 commission for one showing he said, "I no longer feel bad."

The couple knew the agent was likely lying about the inside of the home because the outside was spectacular. Had their agent been honest and not told the couple a lie about the inside of the home, and had he been willing to set up an appointment for them to see the home; they would not have telephoned on their own.

Who knows, I may have agreed to pay more than the $5,000.00 I first offered; or give a one week listing instead of 48-hours but I was not willing to pay as high as 6%.

I cannot stress enough that you must find and work with a reputable agent, one who will represent you to the best of their ability and one who has integrity. Get references and check them to be sure this is the person you want to represent you.

❖

CHAPTER 15

Buying a New Home

Advantages

- Newer homes tend to use an open concept design and with the use of new window technology, it allows the builder to use larger, more energy efficient windows.
- The larger windows allow more sunlight into a room without the loss of warm or cool air (depending on the season) escaping outside.
- You get to select from a wide range of colours, styles and materials for the walls, cabinets, countertops, flooring etc.
- Builders generally sell upgrades to the interior and it is pretty much up to you as to what you want. It can be a luxury kitchen, bathrooms, flooring, finished basements, custom paint or wallpaper, etc.
- New Homes are built to the latest building codes for plumbing, electrical, insulation and in some jurisdictions, especially in cold climate areas, it is mandatory to install at least a medium efficiency furnace, but many builders install a high efficiency furnace because they are 50% more fuel efficient than a conventional furnace. These furnaces are smaller in size, have no chimney, instead they use a small 2 1/2" diameter plastic pipe, which is vented threw an outside wall.
- You will be the first person to live in the house, which for some people it gives greater personal satisfaction.
- Many new homes are built in states or provinces where it is mandatory for a new homebuilder to belong to a New Home Warranty Program.

Check with your province or state to find out if they have such a program.
- Everything is new, so if you have purchased your home from a reputable builder you should expect to enjoy many years without having to pay for replacements or repairs to the windows roof, furnace, plumbing or air conditioning etc.

Disadvantages
- The builder may not be registered with a New Home Warranty Program and therefore you may not have any protection against any major defects in the home.
- Dust and mud are common in new developments and if you happen to be one of the first families to move in you can expect to have this problem for up to 3 years. Keep in mind, there is a lot of noise from the trades' people, their trucks and equipment.
- Many new homes are built in the suburbs and may require longer commute times to the office, hospital or school, which may require your children to get bussed to a school.
- It may be years before you get any strip plazas in your area for local convenience item shopping.
- There may be a delay in the closing date, which could create hardship to you and your families if you are forced to find shelter while you wait, for the house to be finished.
- Most builders do not supply curtain rods and draperies and if they do, they will cost you extra.
- Fencing, landscaping and in some cases the lawn is an extra charge. It is up to you to add these items at a later date and at your expense.
- Goods and Services tax (GST) of 5% is added to the purchase price. (Canada Only) Most builders will include the GST in the selling price. However, be sure that the price you are quoted includes the GST as you don't want to be surprised on closing date.

CHAPTER 16

❖

Buying a Previously Owned Home

Advantages

- No GST to pay unless the home has been substantially renovated. (Canada Only)
- Generally less expensive.
- Already decorated and comes with that lived in feeling.
- May have a unique architectural style that is no longer available at an affordable price from a builder.
- Landscaping is mature and the fencing is usually done.
- The schools are built and usually within walking distance.
- Stores are close by.
- The finished basement and or other extras such as drapery tracks, blinds and fixtures are included in the price.
- Most often appliances are included or offered for sale at the time of selling the home. Don't assume anything, get it in writing.
- The Neighborhood is established and built up.

Disadvantages

- The house is not built to the latest building standards and may have aluminum wiring instead of copper wiring. Lead instead of copper pipes and the house may have urea formaldehyde foam insulation.

- No warranty
- The house may have been renovated by the owner or a handyperson without getting the necessary permits and not to code, which could pose a safety hazard.
- The décor it may not be to your liking and expensive to replace.
- Furnace may be safe and functional; but not efficient.
- Windows and roof tiles may need replacing.
- May have a cracked foundation.
- The basement walls or floor may be leaking and you may need extensive repairs.
- Trees on the property. Make sure that trees, especially mature trees are not planted too close to the foundation. If they are close you may have a problem with roots penetrating the foundation. If trees are close to the foundation make sure that the municipality you live in will allow you to cut down the tree. Some don't!

Note

Paying money for a home inspection is money well spent. It is very important to hire a home inspector, especially on a resale home. You are paying the inspector to uncover any problems but they need to be most diligent when they are looking at the structure, furnace, roof, and plumbing. Also have them inspect for insect problems such as termites or carpenter ants.

CHAPTER 17

❖

Canadian Home Ownership Expenses

New Home

1) If the home is located in Canada, GST will be added to the purchase price of the new. home. At the time of writing this book the cost is 5% of the purchase price. Almost all builders advertise the price of the new home with GST included. Make sure the price you are quoted includes GST.

2) Landscaping charges. Some municipalities insist that the builder supply landscaping such as trees and shrubs on your property, the builder may not tell you how much this charge will be but they must put it in writing that there will be a charge. Read the offer to purchase closely and find out how much these extra charges will cost.

3) Water meter. Depending on where you live, it may be the new homeowners' responsibility to pay for the water meter. Expect to pay approximately $150.00 for the meter.

4) Telephone jacks. The phone line and outlet wiring to the various rooms is provided but you may have to pay for your service hook up and for jack installations. If you do have to pay, expect to pay approximately $350.00 for service.

5) Cable Television wiring. If you have a new home built in a neighborhood that has cable, the homebuilder should install the cable wire. However, the wiring may be installed in a limited number of rooms and it may be your responsibility to pay for additional outlets and to pay for connecting the wire to the jack in the outlet. Expect to pay $25.00 per outlet.

Previously Owned Home

Except for activating your telephone service, contacting the utility companies and getting a change of address from the post office, the previous owner has already paid for the telephone jacks, cable jacks, water meter, landscaping etc.

Expenses Associated with both
New & Previously Owned Homes

1) Appraisal fees: The lender may charge you between $250.00 and $350.00 to have the property appraised. Appraisals are rarely required on new homes.
2) Property survey. If the seller has a recent survey a new survey is unlikely, but if the survey is more than 20 years old then the lender may insist on a new survey, expect to pay $300.00 to $500.00.
3) Home inspection. A home inspection is a detailed report on the condition of the home. The cost can be as much as $300.00 depending on the complexities of the inspection. For example an older home, larger home, or a home that is suspected of having contaminants such as pyrite, radon gas, or urea formaldehyde will cost you more for the inspection.

Many new homebuilders do their own inspections but a few homebuilders use independent home inspectors. Regardless of who inspects the home, you are usually required to be in attendance, before the final closing. The cost of the inspection is usually included in the price of the home. But make sure!

You are the one who hires and pays for the inspection on a resale home so it is entirely up to you whether to attend during the inspection. The report is done in writing and it will give you a detailed summary of any defects.

I recommend that you get references and check them before you hire an inspector. This way you will be more apt to hire a reputable inspector.

When making an offer on a resale home, make it a conditional offer, one where you can get out of the offer without penalty if the inspection were to reveal serious problems.

Some problems may require you to adjust the offering price to reflect what it will cost you to correct the defects, but the defects may be serious enough to cancel the deal and find another home.

4) If the home has a well, you should have the quality of the water tested to ensure that the water supply is adequate and potable.
5) If there is a septic tank make sure it is up to code for your area by having a septic tank and drain field inspection.
6) Estoppel certificate Fee (not applicable in Quebec, Canada) this applies if you are buying a condominium or strata unit and could cost up to $100.00.

Closing Costs

1) Title insurance is a must these days as it will protect you in the event that there are defects in the title to the property. The fee for legal and title insurance is based on a percentage of the properties value but is usually around ¼ to ½% for both. Ask your lawyer for a cost estimate before hiring her.
2) Land registration fees (sometimes called a Land Transfer Tax, Deed Registration Fee, Tariff or Property Purchases Tax) Some provinces and states will charge you this fee at the time of transferring title of the property. The cost is a percentage of the property's purchase price and may vary. Check with your lawyer/notary to see what the current rates are.
3) Prepaid expenses: Expenses such as property taxes, utility bills and filling the oil tank with oil are all prepaid expenses which mean that on closing you will be required to reimburse the seller for any

unused portion of the expense they have paid.

4) Property Insurance: The lender will require this because the home is used as security for the loan. It is a condition for the loan and must be in place at the time of closing. This insurance covers the cost of repairing, rebuilding or replacing your home in the event of fire or other catastrophe. You are not required to insure the contents of the home but the cost for this type of insurance is low and I highly recommend that you have this homeowners insurance.

5) Moving expenses: This cost for a local move can vary from a low of $50.00 if friends or relatives help and you own or have access to a truck, or as much as a $1,500.00 if you hire a professional moving company. Check references and make sure that the moving company does not charge you for circumstances beyond your control, such as a truck breakdown or accident, while on the way to you or traveling to your new home.

6) Make sure that your belongings are insured, in case of an accident or theft along the route to your new home. Contact your broker or insurance company to find out if your homeowner policy will cover your property while in transit. If it is not covered, buy the coverage from the insurance company. Get a quotation from the moving company as well, as they may be cheaper source. Be aware that movers will not take responsibility for items such as jewelry, currency, or important papers.

7) Most financial institutions prefer to be paid monthly and usually at the first of the month. Therefore, they may at the time of transferring the money to the seller i.e. (closing date), insist on being paid for the interest adjustment period. This is the period that they have advanced you the money before the first of the month. If this period is for 15 days then on a $200,000.00 loan at 5.25% interest they will be looking for approximately $450.00.

❖

CHAPTER 18

Selling A Home

In a previous chapter we covered the ins and outs of buying a home but eventually you will sell it and that's what this chapter is all about.

Curb Appeal

Since the first thing anyone sees when he or she first looks at your home is the front of the home it is very important that you make it as appealing as possible. The lawn should be mowed and well maintained by removing those unsightly weeds and filling in any bald patches with sod or at the very least grass seed. It's also a good idea to plant fresh flowers and trim or add any shrubs as required. Doing these little things will cost next to nothing but it will give the front of the home that cared-for look. If necessary, give the front a face-lift, with a fresh coat of paint.

Remove Excess Furniture & Clean Your Closets

Most of us have too much furniture for the size of the room. If you have ever gone through a decorated model home, you know what I mean. The interior designers of these models homes keep furniture to a minimum. They usually do not show a dresser and if they do show one, it is normally small and the master bedroom almost never has more than one dresser in the room.

I don't want you to get carried away because you still need to live in the home, while you are trying to sell it. I do however, want you to remove and place into storage any and all unnecessary furniture.

Tidy up those closets so that when the buyers view them, they have a neat and orderly appearance. Do not give the prospective buyer the impression that you are placing their life in danger when they open the closet door. Here again store the excess in a box or suitcase in the basement, at a friends place or at a rented storage locker.

Neutral Paint

Painted walls can look great and cost about a ¼ of the price of wallpaper. Paint is also something that with care and patience any handy person can do a good job.

Studies have shown that most people prefer that a painted wall be in a neutral colour such as soft white or beige. If you can afford it, have an interior designer help you to make the choice. Stay away from any loud colours that you or your kids may love but not necessarily a prospective buyer.

Facets And Door Handles

This is a very inexpensive way to spruce up your home for a nominal cost. Replace those doors handles that no longer shine because the brass plating has worn off.

Facets and door handles can be bought quite cheaply at your local store and they most likely will have people on staff that will be more than happy to explain how to install them.

If you can't do it yourself, then hire a home handy person to install them for you. This small change can make a bathroom look great and may be all that you need to make those bath or kitchen areas come alive with a clean, fresh and well-maintained look.

Outside Photographs Of Your Home For Advertising Purposes

Make sure that any photos used for the purpose of selling your home, such as photos used in an advertisement or on a specification sheet are always of a current season and not from a previous season.

Why?

Because if the photo is from a season other than the current one, it will get your home the kind of attention that you do not want. You do not want prospective buyers to think that your home has been on the market for a long period of time and that there may be something wrong with it.

Photograph Package

If the home is located in an area where you get winter, especially where you get snow, place photographs in a binder on the kitchen table of how the yard, decking, pond, pool, gazebo and gardens look in the summer time. Doing this will add to the salability of the home and give the prospective buyer a taste of what is yet to come. Be sure to place a note on the binder asking the prospective buyer to leave the binder behind when they leave, otherwise you may need a lot of binders.

Feature Sheet On The Home

If your real-estate agent does not do this, then I suggest you put something together that you can leave on the kitchen counter for all prospective buyers to take with them after they have visited your home. It is a very inexpensive touch.

This sheet should list all the upgrades that the home has to offer. The list should outline the details regarding a finished basement or an entertainment room, gazebo, hot tub, upgraded kitchen or bathroom. In other words list anything that will give the new owner a benefit or feature over and above basics. Don't make the list too long but do list all the added benefits and features of the home.

Also, include a photo of the front of the home. If you have a computer and a digital camera it is easy to download the photo from your camera and print it directly onto the spec sheet but if not, then glue a photo to the top of the specification sheet and list the above-mentioned items below the photo.

Another feature you may add to this spec sheet is a layout of the rooms and if you can, include the room sizes. If the home is small it may be best to leave the room sizes off as it could hurt the selling price or salability of the home. Where you display these spec sheets leave a little sign, inviting the prospective buyer to take a spec sheet, with them.

Creative Financing

To avoid having to lower the price of the home and to get a faster sale you may if your finances permit help the buying decision along by lending the buyer money.

As with any loan, the people borrowing the money must be credit worthy because the last thing you want is to chase people for money. If the people are credit worthy it is most likely that you would be repaid on time as promised but as an added precaution you must register a mortgage or deed of trust.

Miscellaneous;

The last couple of points I have are:
1) Leave the home when your agent is showing it to prospective buyers. Go to the store, around the block or out for dinner but be sure to allow enough time for them to finish their walk through without them having to feel rushed.
2) If you're looking for a quick sale increase the amount of commission the selling agent can earn if they sell the home in less than 30 to 45 days. This will give them the extra incentive to work the listing a little harder.

CHAPTER 19

❖

North American Mortgages

T he next several chapters deal with mortgages and deeds of trust. Canada and the United States of America have many similarities when it comes to our banking systems and the way in which credit is loaned to all of us. In this book I discuss both because many Americans and Canadians buy properties in each of our respective countries.

Canadians and Americans trade with each other all the time. Our spoken English is the same with little or no accent. Our laws, though not completely the same are for all practical purposes similar.

Remember although there are similarities when you purchase property always be sure to hire a lawyer in the state or province where you are buying the property.

Why?

Because the lawyers where you are buying the property are experts in the law for that local. It is also a good idea to seek professional advice from a lawyer, real estate expert and in some cases an accountant. There may be tax advantages or disadvantages that you should be made aware of so I suggest you find an expert one that specializes in the local where the property is located.

Although our mortgages are similar they are not the same and for this reason I have written chapters, for Canadians and Americans. Many States in the USA don't use mortgages but they do use a deed of trust. The end purpose is the same but it is different than a mortgage and I have explained what these differences are.

Where the information is unique to the USA or Canada I have headed the chapter as such. If the information is the same for both our countries I have headed the chapter with the topic only.

Now let's get started!

❖

CHAPTER 20

Reverse Mortgage or Reverse Deed of Trust

W e have talked in great length about how to get a mortgage or (deed of trust, USA only) with the best terms, terms that will save you the most money. Now I want to talk about a reverse mortgage or reverse deed of trust.

I am sure you have seen advertisements on television offering you a chance to get your hands on the equity that you have built in your home over the years. It sure looks easy and it sure is appealing to those who are short of cash. You can apply for a reverse mortgage if you are at least 60-years of age in Canada and at least 62-years of age in the United States and own your home.

A reverse mortgage is a mortgage or deed of trust that has the same clauses, terms and conditions as any other mortgage or deed of trust, except that this mortgage requires no payments until you, move, sell the home or pass away. Does the not having to make payments part of this sound good?

Yes it sounds great.

So what is the catch?

There are number of them. First, the interest rate you will be charged is 2 to 2 ½% higher than a regular first mortgage.

The main reason for this difference is that as long as you live you can remain in the home and without making any mortgage payments regardless of where the value of your home goes, up or down you don't have to move because of the value, even if the home ends up being worth less than the amount of the loan.

The second catch is, there is no going back. Once you have agreed to the deal, you can't change your mind unless you pay all the money back, including the interest that gets added to the amount you borrowed.

For example if you took a $200,000 loan against the value of your home at 8.5% interest, after just 10 years, you would owe the lender approximately $460,000.00. This is a lot of money to repay.

It's not necessary to take the money in a lump sum. You could arrange to have it paid to you monthly or you could arrange a line of credit and draw on the money as you need it. The money you receive is not taxable as it is your own money or equity being returned to you.

Unless your home increases in value at a rate greater than the interest cost you will have racked up, then this reverse mortgage will eat away at your equity.

Now suppose your health were to change for the worse and it became necessary for you to leave your home and live in a retirement home. You are obligated to repay the amount you borrowed plus interest when you move.

To me the name reverse mortgage implies that you are taking a step backwards. I am not saying that a reverse mortgage is completely a bad thing but I am saying that you need to evaluate all the advantages and disadvantages of taking a reverse mortgage.

Another option would be to take a small mortgage on the property and repay it from your retirement income. If this is not going to give you enough money or the mortgage payment is too high for you to handle the payments, then consider selling the home and move to a smaller home.

By doing this you may find considerable savings in utility costs and property taxes. With the money you will have left after the sale and purchase of another home you should consider the purchase of an annuity as it will give you an income for the rest of your life. Talk to a financial advisor for more details.

I don't want to scare you but if you have a spouse or significant other whom you share life with make sure that you have a last survivor clause in the reverse mortgage or reverse deed of trust agreement.

This means that no matter who dies first the other person can remain in the home under the same circumstances as I outlined previously.

A reverse mortgage may be exactly what you need, but before you sign anything check with a independent financial advisor who does not have a financial interest in what you are signing and also check with your lawyer.

❖

CHAPTER 21

Canadian Mortgage

Only a few people are fortunate enough to have enough money to pay for their home in full without the need to borrow money. If you can't pay for the home in full, then you will need to borrow money. The mortgagee (lender) will lend you the money, charge you interest, and register a mortgage against the property until the mortgage (loan) is repaid. Simple? You bet it is.

What is a Mortgage?

A mortgage (loan) is a contract between two parties, one party who wants to borrow the money and one party whose wish is to lend money. The borrower is referred to as the "mortgagor" and the lender is referred to as the "mortgagee". This contract stipulates a specific property, typically a residence, building or land as collateral for a loan and this contract is registered on file to give the lender complete security.

Once a mortgage is filed; it gives the mortgagee the right if they have not been paid to force the sale of the property. Typically a mortgagee (lender) will not start any proceedings to sell the property until they have exhausted all reasonable options with the mortgagor (borrower).

Types of Mortgages

There are many different types of mortgages such as reverse, blanket, lease-hold and construction mortgages; but my focus in this book is on the mortgage for your residence.

Canadian mortgages are "recourse" mortgages. This means, if the lender has not been paid in full from the amount they received from the forced sale of the home plus repaid for their expenses for lawyers, court costs, selling the home, arrears interest owing and penalty charges the lender can file a claim against the borrower. Saskatchewan is the only province where the lender cannot go after the borrowers other assets or future earnings.

This claim may very well allow the lender to seize the borrowers other assets and force the sale of those assets. If the lender is still owed any money after the asset sale they could still go after the borrower's future earnings until the loan is paid in full.

In the United States of America many of the mortgages and deeds of trust are non-recourse. In a nut shell, a mortgage that is non-recourse means that mortgagor (borrower) can just walk away from the property and not be held responsible for a shortfall in the amount of money the lender receives from the sale of the property.

Conventional Mortgage

This is the most common type of financing for a principal residence. Its terms and conditions are standard. Most banks, including credit unions, offer conventional mortgages.

Federal legislation in Canada prohibits a bank from lending more than 80% of the purchase price unless the borrower has mortgage insurance for the full value of the mortgage.

In order to qualify for a conventional mortgage you will need a down payment equal to or greater than 20% of the appraised value. The appraised value is in most cases, the purchase price and if you're lucky enough to find a home where the appraised value is more than the purchase price then that will make it a better investment.

Usually this 20% rule is sufficient for the banks or credit unions to agree to lend the money without insisting on mortgage insurance.

However, occasionally a lender may still require insurance. For example if the property is located in areas that will take a long time to sell or the value of the home is declining rapidly.

High Ratio Mortgage

This type of mortgage does not have a minimum down payment rule because you must have mortgage insurance from a reputable company in order to get this mortgage.

Mortgage Insurance

These two insurers are both excellent sources for mortgage insurance and can be reached at.

1) Canada Mortgage and Housing@ 1-800-668-2642 or @ www.cmhc.ca

2) Genworth Financial Canada@ 1-800-511-8888, or @ www.genworth.ca

There are other sources for insurance other than the two I have shown above but I recommend that you check with your lender as they may have a preference as to whom they would prefer you to use.

The purpose of the insurance is to encourage the banks and credit unions to lend money to those individuals who have the income to make the mortgage payments but do not have a 20% down payment.

It also encourages the bank or credit union to loan money to those people, who they might otherwise decline because of the inherent risk of seasonal employment_or they may be employed in an industry that runs a major risk of permanent layoff.

Other lenders might be more accommodating but the cost to the borrower would be much higher.

Why?

Because of the risk.

The insurance protects the lender, if, in the unlikely event the borrower does not repay the loan; the insurance provider will repay it plus all arrears, interest charges, penalties, and any other expenses the lender would incur to sell the property, such as, real estate fees, legal fees, etc.

A high ratio mortgage will cost you more, because of the added cost of the insurance premium. The premium for the insurance is paid on closing but the lender will usually add the cost to the mortgage. Make sure your lender, is willing to do this, otherwise you will need to have the funds for the insurance premium on closing day.

How Much Does Mortgage Insurance Cost?

Coverage is not automatic but in most cases the lender will apply on your behalf. There is usually an application fee, which in most cases the lender will pay and recharge you. The insurance can cost as little as .5% up to 2.9% before surcharges. These rates may have changed since this book was published, so I suggest you visit their websites for the current rates.

For example, on a $300,000.00 home with a 5% down payment the insurance will cost you 2.9% of the mortgage amount, for a 25-year or less amortization period. If the period is 25 to 30-years expect to pay a premium of .20% and if the period is 30 to 35-years you will pay a premium of .40%. This will mean on a 35-year amortization you will pay 3.30%. At 3.30% the insurance premium would cost $9,900.00.

The larger your down payment, the less your insurance premium will be. Using the same $300,000.00 value and a down payment of 10%, the premium would be 2%, giving a total cost of $6,000.00.

Ontario and Quebec require that you pay provincial sales tax on the insurance premium and you must pay this, at the time of closing. In most cases the lender will not add the provincial sales tax to the mortgage, so make sure you have the money and put it away for closing day.

Both Genworth and CMHC for a small additional fee will in most cases allow you the option of mortgage portability; but check with your lender to be sure the mortgage you are considering, is a mortgage that is portable and can be transferred to your next home.

Some lenders give the portability option, but you must start the loan on the new property within 30 to 60 days. On average people move every 6 ½ years, this feature could save you from having to re-purchase insurance if you were to move before the mortgage was paid in full.

Can You Avoid The Insurance?

You may be able to avoid this insurance by taking a second mortgage on the property in order to meet the 20% down payment rule; but unless this second mortgage is for a short period of time, the interest cost, will most likely exceed the cost of the insurance.

Why?

Because the second mortgage lender will want a much higher interest rate than the first mortgage lender.

If you do choose to use the second mortgage option and the term of the second mortgage expires after the first mortgage, be sure it contains a post-ponement clause. Without this clause you would not be able to renew or replace the first mortgage when it became due until the second mortgage holder gave you permission. In other words, without the second mortgage holders' permission your first mortgage holder would most likely not agree to renew or replace the mortgage and if they did agree it would most likely be at second mortgage interest rate.

Why?

Mortgages are not titled first, second, third they become first, second and third from the date they are registered. Whoever registers first is first. Be sure to discuss this with your lawyer.

How Many Mortgages Can You Have?

You can have as many mortgages as there are lenders willing to lend you the money; but if the first mortgage interest rate is 4.5%, you can expect the second mortgage rate to be approximately 10%, a third at roughly 13% and a fourth as high as 20%. The reason the interest rate rises for each additional mortgage is the additional risk the lender is taking. If there is a foreclosure and sale of the property the first mortgage holder must be fully paid before any monies are paid to the second, third or fourth mortgagee.

Title Insurance?

"Title insurance protects you the homeowner from fraudulent claims against your property." This type of insurance will protect you against any defects in the title of the property, such as a charges or claims that have not yet been filed or that were filed but not picked up by the searches made by the lawyer before ownership passed to you. Title insurance could also cover you for a mortgage that remains on title, although it was discharged and paid out.

The electronic age, has made stealing your identity a little easier for professional thieves. Identity theft is becoming more of a problem every day. The first step is to steal your identity then by using fake identification they fraudulently borrow money in your name by forging your signature, obtain the funds and then disappear and you are left with the responsibility of paying a lawyer to reclaim title to your property.

The legal cost and stress can be a lot to overcome but with the correct type of title insurance you will have peace of mind at least in knowing that the legal cost would be paid for by insurance. One other feature of this insurance is that coverage begins when you take title and it will continue until you sell your home. Your lawyer is a good place to find out more details and the cost of this "Title Insurance".

❖

CHAPTER 22

How Canadians Can Borrow Money From TheirRegistered Retirement Savings Plan (RRSP)

How to Borrow Money for a Down Payment from your RRSP

If you are a first time homebuyer, or you or your spouse have not owned an owner occupied home (residence) for a period of 5-years you qualify. Also neither you nor your spouse can own the home more than 30-days before the RRSP withdrawal.

If you meet this criterion and if you have the funds in yours or your spouses RRSP plan you may withdraw up to the maximum allowable limit of $25,000.00. You can't withdraw more than you have in your RRSP and any contributions made to the RRSP during the year of withdrawing the money are not eligible for withdrawal.

The money is removed from your RRSP account with the understanding that you have an agreement to purchase or build a qualifying home. The home is bought or built by October 1 of the year following the year in which you've received the funds from the RRSP. You may be able to get an extension if you can show extenuating circumstances. The money must be fully repaid into the RRSP account within 15-years.

The repayments must start in the second calendar year following the calendar year of the RRSP withdrawal and be at least 1/15th of the amount you withdrew. Any payment made in the first 60 days of a year count as repayments for the previous year.

Withdrawal Example:
If you make a withdrawal in 2009; you must begin making payments no later than March 1, 2012.If you fail to deposit 1/15th of the amount in any of the 15 years, then that amount becomes taxable to you for the year(s) of default. You may increase the amount or frequency of your payments at any time and thus shorten the amount of time to repay the amount you withdrew.

If your spouse or common law partner has contributed $25,000.00 to an RRSP, then under the same rules they are also entitled to borrow up to a maximum of $25,000.00.

For more details on if you qualify visit the Revenue Canada web site.

How to Borrow Money for a Mortgage from Your RRSP

If you have sufficient funds in your RRSP you can lend yourself the money and using real estate as security, usually your principal residence. It does not have to be your residence you could use the money for financing a new business but the loan must be issued and be approved by the mortgage insurer for that purpose. The Canada Mortgage and Housing Corporation does not allow equity take out loans. You will need to find another mortgage insurer such as Genworth.

There are conditions and the first condition is that a public mortgage insurer such as the Canada Mortgage and Housing Corporation or Genworth Financial insures the mortgage. Another condition is, the mortgage must have normal commercial terms and you must charge yourself the current interest rate offered by the banks.

❖

CHAPTER 23

Canadian Mortgage Terms
& Amortization Period

Mortgage Term

A mortgage term is the period of time (life of the mortgage); until the term has ended. Mortgage terms are generally as short as 6-months and as long as 10-years or more. When the term has ended, the mortgage matures; which means the entire amount owing on the mortgage is due and payable to the lender. There are no additional interest charges or other charges as long as the monies are paid on the date they are due.

If the mortgage can't be paid in full by the borrower on this date, then it is time to renegotiate the rate of interest the lender will lend the money to the borrower at and the length of time on the new mortgage term.

Contrary to popular belief the lender is under no obligation to continue lending you the money at the end of the term. Most major lenders are more than willing to grant another mortgage term but they have no legal obligation to do so!

Why would they not renew?

If they are a small company or a private lender they may now need the money or perhaps they merely wish to get out of the lending business. If you have a history of late payments or missed payments, then they may consider you to be a high risk, a risk they are not willing to continue a relationship with.

Amortization Period

The amortization period is the period of time it will take to repay the mortgage in full. A typical mortgage has a 5-year term and a 25-year amortization period and for generations we have accepted this as the norm; but it need not be. A small increase in your monthly payment or a lump sum payment made annually will cut the amortized life of the mortgage by years and it will reduce the interest cost by thousands of dollars. Amortization periods of up to 35-years are available but if at all possible stay away from these loans as they will cost you plenty, both in time and money.

Shop carefully for your mortgage, and review the following examples as they highlight what different mortgage terms can cost.

Shira and Steven borrowed $200,000.00 on a 5-year term, amortized over 35-years at 4.50% interest. Assuming that the interest rate would remain at 4.50% over the 35-year amortized period and assuming their mortgage payments would always be paid on time, they will pay $195,375.40 in interest and their monthly payment will be $941.37 per month, for 420-months.

Frank and Bobby borrowed $200,000.00 on a 5-year fixed term, amortized over 25-years at 4.50% interest. Using the same assumptions as Shira and Steven, Frank and Bobby will be making payments of $1,106.95 per month for 300-months and will end up paying the lender, $132,083.78 in interest charges.

Toni and Bill borrowed $200,000.00 at 4.50% interest, on a 22-year amortization. Again using the same assumptions as Shira and Steven, Toni and Bill's monthly payment will be $1,190.19. By paying $83.24 more per month than Frank and Bobby they will pay their mortgage off 3-years sooner.

Their interest cost will be $114,210.38 over the 22-year term but that little extra amount of $83.24 a month will save them $17,873.40 in interest compared to Frank and Bobby and a whopping saving of $81,165.02 compared to Shira and Steven.

❖

CHAPTER 24

Canadian Mortgage Options

There are basically two options for mortgages; open and closed. An open mortgage means that you the mortgagor (borrower) have the right to prepay the mortgage at anytime without giving any notice, or having to pay any penalty interest or bonus.

The mortgage may contain a clause insisting that any prepayment be made on the same date as your regular mortgage payment and the lender may require a 30-day notice.

Open mortgages are not as popular as closed because it is a more expensive way to borrow money. An open mortgage can cost you as much as 1% to 2% more than a closed mortgage.

Closed mortgages are the most common.

Why?

Because the lender (mortgagee) is now in a position to charge you 3-months' bonus interest at the interest rate chargeable under the terms of the mortgage, on the amount you prepay or they can charge you the interest rate differential (IRD), whichever is greater. We will discuss prepayment options in more detail later. Why do lenders charge you for the privilege that allows you to pay your loan before the end of the term?

A mortgage is a contract and under basic contract law, if one party to a contract breaches said contract then the other party is entitled to be put in the same position, as they would have been; had there been no breach of contract. Therefore, if you pay the mortgage off before end of the term, you have breached the contract and you must adequately compensate the lender for their loss by putting them into the same position, as they would have been in, had there been no breach.

Variable Rate Mortgage

This type of mortgage is available in both open and closed. A variable rate mortgage is tied to the prime rate of interest. When your financial institution quotes you a variable interest rate it is most often quoted at prime plus or minus. They will usually give you the option of changing the variable to a fixed interest rate at any time during the variable mortgage term, for the balance of the mortgage term you selected.

In periods of declining interest rates a variable rate mortgage is excellent because if the interest rate goes down and your payment remains the same your principal amount of the mortgage will decrease faster, and so will your cost of interest.

Stay away from a variable rate mortgage in a period of rising interest rates. A variable rate mortgage comes with what is called a trigger point. There are usually 2 trigger points, the first trigger point is usually set at 2% above the interest rate you agreed to at the time of closing the mortgage and the mortgage payment is set at the amount of payment (providing the interest rate remained the same over the entire amortized period) necessary to pay the mortgage in full over the amortized period you selected which as we previously discussed may be for a period of 25-years.

Since the rate is tied to prime, if the prime rate were to increase by more than 2% you will have reached the trigger point and at this point your payment will be increased.

Variable rate Example:
Susan has a 5-year variable rate mortgage, with a 25-year amortized term. Her monthly payment on a $200,000.00 mortgage at 6.00% is $1,279.61 per month. If the interest rate increases to 8.25%, Susan's bank would activate the trigger and her monthly payment would increase to $1,558.46 per month. I know, you don't think that this is likely but if it did happen to you, could you handle the volatility?

If the interest rate Susan was being charged increased to 7.00% a month, after just two months into her variable rate mortgage term; then the trigger point would not be reached, and her payment would not automatically increase. She would need to request an increase.

How would she know?

Whenever the prime rate of interest changes, the lender would notify her of the change, in writing and they would suggest that she adjust her payment.

All changes to the prime interest rate either up or down are announced on the radio and television as well as in the newspapers. Lenders would prefer that mortgage payments be kept the same.

Why?

Well because, over the 5-year term and assuming no changes and that the interest rate remained at 7%, Susan would pay approximately $65,093.85 in interest, which is $10,618.12, more than if the rate remained at 6.00%.

Keep in mind that this $10,618.12 is now an interest expense and the principal amount of her mortgage will be $10,618.12 higher than it would have been if the interest rate had remained at 6% or she had increased her monthly payment by $120.64.This 1 % difference will add years to Susan's 25-year amortized period.

There is a second trigger point and this one is to prevent your principal amount of the mortgage from getting too large. On conventional mortgages if at any time the outstanding principal amount (including deferred interest) exceeds 80% of the fair market value of the mortgaged property as determined by the lender (with or without an appraisal), such amount being the trigger point the lender will give notice to the borrower of the excess and within 30-days of receiving the notice the borrower must make a lump sum payment to the lender at least equal to the amount of the trigger point excess; or the borrower must get an appraisal of the properties fair market value at their expense and if this value shows the mortgage to be less than the 80% trigger point then the borrower need not make a lump sum payment.

On high ratio mortgages if at any time the outstanding principal amount (including deferred interest) exceeds the trigger point by 105% of the original principal amount, the lender will give the borrower notice of such excess (the trigger point excess) and within 30 days the borrower must do one of the following:

i) make a lump sum payment to the lender to reduce the outstanding principal amount by an amount equal to the trigger point excess;

ii) agree with the lender to convert the mortgage to a fixed rate mortgage; or

iii) increase the amount of each regular installment of Principal and interest to an amount sufficient to amortize the outstanding principal amount including deferred interest over the remaining amortized period.

The trigger points are not there to protect you; they are there to protect the lender. They want to be certain that they could recover their money in the event of default on the mortgage payments.

The example I gave above regarding the additional interest cost to the borrower and the longer period of time it will take for the borrower to repay the mortgage would not activate the second trigger, in a period of rising property values.

Remember the lender is out to make as much money as possible with little or no risk and your job is to save as much money as possible. So pay attention to the interest rates you are charged and if rates go up, increase your mortgage payment.

Fixed Rate Mortgage

A fixed rate mortgage offers the borrower comfort in knowing that the interest rate they will be borrowing money, is fixed for the term of the mortgage. If the term is 6-months or 10-years it matters not. It is fixed for the term.

A term can be as short as 6-months and it is the least expensive option because the lender is committing their money for a short period of time.

In fact, most borrowers opt for the 5-year term even though if you look at mortgage rates over the last 25-years it shows that you would have saved far more money in interest charges by going short. Short terms are not for the meek, because sometimes the volatility is more than most are willing to cope with.

I will remind you, most people move on average every 6-½ years and since there is a penalty interest charge of at least 3-months interest (more on this later) on the amount of the prepayment, then why would you want to renew for a second term of 5-years. If you can't handle the volatility of a short term then take a 5-year term for the first term and then after you are comfortable with the interest rate and your mortgage payment; take a 6-month or 1-year term thereafter. This way you can time your move with the mortgage term and save yourself a lot of money.

❖

CHAPTER 25

Canadian Portable Mortgage

What Is A Portable Mortgage?

A portable mortgage is a mortgage that you can take with you from one home to another. It is an excellent idea, because it provides flexibility to borrowers with a long-term mortgage to transfer the mortgage to their next residence without paying the 3-month or Interest Rate Differential (IRD) penalty.

Also, as previously mentioned, if you have a high ratio mortgage and will again have a high ratio mortgage you can also avoid having to pay for the insurance again. Yes, there is a premium to the insurance rate for the portability privilege but it is nominal compared with having to pay for the insurance over again.

When negotiating the portability feature be sure to add a feature that will allow you to blend the existing mortgage with a new mortgage. The new money is the money that would be borrowed in addition to the old mortgage money, thereby allowing you to add money to the old mortgage in order to afford the new home.

Usually the new money would be loaned at the interest rate in effect at the time of borrowing the money and it would be blended with the old money interest rate to come up with a new weighted average rate.

This rate would remain until the balance of the term, which would be the amount of time remaining on the old mortgage.

Blended interest Example:

If you had $120,000 remaining on the mortgage at the time of taking $80,000.00 in new money, you will have 60% of the new loan of $200,000.00 at the old interest rate of 6% and 40% of the new loan at 5%.

$$6\% \text{ times } 60\% = 3.60\%$$
$$5\% \text{ times } 40\% = 2.00\%$$

$$\text{Total} = 5.60\%$$

Although this new weighted average interest rate is higher than what the new interest rate of 5% is, it may still save considerable money because you avoid any prepayment penalty and having to pay for the mortgage insurance again.

Remember that this is a prepayment privilege and not an obligation. You do not need to go this route; in fact if your circumstances were to change and you had enough money to purchase your next home with a down payment of at least 20%, then you would not need to purchase mortgage insurance. The cost of prepaying to discharge the mortgage sooner would most likely cost less than the extra .60% interest for the blended rate.

The only way you will know for sure is to do the math!

As with other mortgage terms, you must however, negotiate this portability option at the time of taking out the mortgage because it is not automatic.

❖

CHAPTER 26

Canadian Prepayment Privileges & Penalties

Prepayment Privileges

Prepayment privileges are an excellent feature to include in any mortgage and it is absolutely essential for borrowers to get the best prepayment privileges that they can.

Three Different Ways to Prepay A Mortgage

1) Lump sum payment
2) Increase your payment amount
3) Make your payments more often

Lump Sum

When shopping for a mortgage don't just look at the interest rate, look at the prepayment options the lender is offering. Most lenders will allow you to prepay up to 15% of the original mortgage amount once per calendar year without penalty or bonus. In many cases they will not allow you to exercise this option if it means that you would be paying the balance of the mortgage in full.

In October of year two of their mortgage, Frank's mother gave Frank and Bobby $70,000.00. They wanted to use this money to pay down their mortgage without having to pay any penalty or interest charges.

Frank and Bobby originally borrowed $200,000.00 and since their mortgage had a 15% prepayment option, they could make a prepayment of

$30,000.00. So on October 1, Frank notified the lender, in writing, that Bobby and he wished to pay down the loan on his next regular payment date by $30,000.00, which happened to be November 1.

On December 1, Frank notified the lender that he wished to pay another $30,000.00 on January 1. Frank satisfied the condition of the loan, by making one pre-payment in one calendar year and another pre-payment in the following calendar year.

Increased Payment Amount

Most lenders will allow you, once a year to increase your payment by up to 100% of the original payment (this is the payment you first started with) for the balance of the mortgage term, a few may insist on 30-days notice but most will do it with as little as 10-days notice.

This benefit is excellent, as the full amount of the extra payment will reduce the principal amount owing, it will also lower your total interest cost and it will reduce the number of years remaining to pay off the mortgage.

One word of caution though, if your financial circumstances were to change, you need to have the option to lower your payments back down, to the original payment amount, without getting charged any fees or penalties.

I suggest that you start with the 25-year amortization term and after a year, increase their monthly payments by the amount of inflation for that year and continue increasing the payment each year thereafter. Doing it this way rather than having too high of a monthly payment to begin with allows you the option of lowering the payment back to the original payment amount if financial circumstances were to change.

Earlier I wrote that Toni and Bill had a mortgage amortized over 22-years and that Frank and Bobby's mortgage is amortized over 25-years. I also said "never make yourself mortgage poor, by paying more than you can comfortably afford." Frank and Bobby opted for the 25-year amortized period but they intend to increase their monthly payment by at least 5% each calendar year.

Where will they get the money?

Both Frank and Bobby receive annual raises in the first quarter of every year and they intend to increase their monthly mortgage payment by the amount they receive from their pay increases.

Why?

Well they want to save money on their interest expense, pay their mortgage off sooner and achieve financial independence sooner.

After they pay off their mortgage they intend to add the money they now spend on the mortgage to their other investments. This plan of monthly investing will give them a high comfort level knowing that they will be financially secure going into retirement years.

Earlier I gave an example of Frank and Bobby's lump sum payments, now let me give you an example of what would happen when they increase their mortgage payment.

Remember, Frank and Bobby's goal was to pay down their mortgage by $70,000.00 and since they have already taken advantage of the 15% pre-payment option in the last 2 calendar years, they can't make another lump sum pre-payment without having to pay an interest penalty, for another calendar year.

They can however, fulfill their goal by doubling their monthly payment until they have paid the remaining $10,000.00 at which time they can lower the payment back down to the original amount they were paying.

Pay More Often

By making your mortgage payment more often than monthly you will reduce the principal amount owing, the interest cost and the amortized period of the mortgage. The trick here is to take the payment required per month and divide it by 4, to arrive at your weekly amount. By doing it this way, you will end up making the equivalent of one extra months' payment per year.

Don't be fooled by a lender taking the monthly payment amount and multiplying it by 12 and then dividing by 52. Yes your payment will be weekly but the gain will be negligible because over the 12-months you will have paid the same amount and the slight gain only comes from the fact that they have received the money a little sooner than waiting a month.

For example, if the monthly payment is $1,100.00 per month and you multiply it by 12, you get $13,200.00 and then divide by 52 you end up with $253.85 per week and then multiply it by 52 weeks you get $13,200.20. Almost the same amount.

Now take the monthly payment of $1,100.00 and divide it by 4 and you get $275.00 as your weekly payment. Multiply this by 52, you will end up with a total amount of $14,300.00 for the year. This means you will have paid $1,100.00 more off the amount owing plus a little extra because of the interest savings.

Prepayment Penalty

As previously discussed mortgage lenders will not allow the borrower to pay the mortgage off in full or any part of it, without paying an interest penalty. Prepayments can only be made if you have prepayment privileges. (*See prepayment section*)

This penalty is for an amount equal to the greater of 3-months' interest at the interest rate chargeable on the mortgage on the amount being prepaid; or the interest rate differential (IRD).

This IRD is basically the difference in the interest rate that the borrower would be paying at the time of prepayment of the principal and the present interest rate that the lender could loan the money at. So does this suggest that if rates were higher at the time of the prepayment that the lender would share the extra money they would earn with the borrower?

Hardly!

If the lender were to earn less than they were earning from the borrower at the time the borrower made the prepayment, then the borrower would be charged the difference in the rate that the lender could earn for the balance of the mortgage term. If they were paying 6% interest and the present market rate is 5%, then the IRD amount would be 1%.

Frank and Bobby are considering paying the balance owing on their mortgage. They have been making their mortgage payments for the last 3-years and have a present principal balance of $188,530.87. The interest rate that the lender can now charge is 1% less than Frank and Bobby are paying.

If the lender were to loan the money out on the same day at 5% then for the next 2-years they would earn $18,285.33 but if Frank and Bobby were to continue paying for the next 2 years at 6% the lender would earn $21,853.26. This means that the lender would earn $3,567.93 less.

Under the 3-month interest rate penalty clause the lender would receive approximately $2,870.00; but, the lender is entitled to be paid the higher of the two amounts which means the lender is entitled to the IRD amount of $3,567.93.

CHAPTER 27

❖

Canadian RRSP Contribution Versus Paying Down Your Mortgage Or Depositing Into A TFSA

Have you ever wondered whether it is better to contribute to your Registered Retirement Savings Plan (RRSP) or pay down your mortgage? First let me start by saying that both are good choices.

How can they both be good choices?

Easy, you see any kind of savings plan for your future is a good choice. Now let's talk about the best choice. In my opinion it is best to pay your mortgage off first and as soon as you possibly can preferably at the same time save money in a TFSA (see chapter 4) and then contribute to your RRSP.

Why?

In Canada mortgage interest is not tax deductible. What this means is that for every dollar you save in interest gives you a dollar increase in your net worth. In other words you are increasing the equity in your home by every dollar you save in interest.

The new TFSA account is a great way to earn money on your contributions tax-free. However, today's earning power on safe investments is so low that you would do much better by paying down the amount owing on your mortgage and save after tax money on the interest charges.

Although you would do better financially by paying down your mortgage I recommend that you also start a TFSA. *(See chapters on the TFSA account and emergency funds.)*

Contributing to an RRSP does not remove the tax owing on the money you deposited into your RRSP account but what it does do is defer the tax to some future date when you will be taxed on all the money in the account.

When?

At the time you withdraw the money from the account.

If you contributed to an RRSP when you were in a 30% tax bracket and later withdrew the funds when you were in a 45% tax bracket you would end up paying more taxes than you saved when you made the contribution.

Let's say you have an emergency in 5-years time and you need to get your hands on $40,000.00 in a hurry. If you placed your money in an RRSP instead of paying extra on your mortgage or depositing the money into your TFSA you would be forced to withdraw the funds from the RRSP.

Why?

Because most lenders will not lend you money on your RRSP's. They don't like RRSP's as collateral. Interesting though they will lend you money over a 12-month period to buy it in the first place.

If you withdrew $40,000.00 from your RRSP account and if at the time of the withdrawal you were in a 45% tax bracket the $40,000.00 withdrawal would get added to your income in the year of the withdrawal and you would need an additional $18,000.00 to cover the taxes.

If you had deposited $5,000.00 each year in your TFSA account over a 4-year period you would have $20,000.00 plus the income earned over the years. You are now in the position to withdraw the full $20,000.00 and still have a balance in the account.

If you also paid down your mortgage by $5,000.00 per year and assuming your home was worth the same as it was 4 years ago, you could rearrange your mortgage, place an additional mortgage on the property, or get a line of credit for the additional $20,000.00 you would need. Doing it this way you would avoid paying taxes, because loans are not taxable.

In Canada your principle residence is one of the best assets for tax purposes that you can own.

Why?

Because any increase in value is tax-free. If your residence increased in value by 6% a year, you will earn the full 6% when the home is eventually sold.

Let's say your money is invested in an RRSP and you are earning 5%. You won't have to pay any income tax on the 5% earnings when you earn it but you will be taxed at your marginal tax rate when you withdraw the money from the plan.

Since most people keep their RRSP money in mutual funds and most buy these funds at their bank they are actually earning a net of 2 to 3% not 5 %.

Why?

Because the bank will charge you a yearly management fee of 2% or more, whether they have earned it or not. When the fund goes up more than market average they have earned it; but if it does not perform as well as the average they have not earned it but they still charge it.

The original thought behind RRSP a contribution was this, when you retired you could withdraw money and pay tax at a lower marginal tax rate. Good idea at the time but most people, especially those without a pension plan are now working much longer than age 65. They have no desire to retire unless they are forced to because of bad health.

Whether your working or not, at age 71 you will be required by Revenue Canada to either

1) Transfer the funds to a Registered Retirement Income Fund (RRIF) and start making withdrawals from this fund. These withdrawals especially if you are still working are what will keep you in the upper tax bracket. There is a formula that outlines how much money you are required to withdraw on an annual basis or
2) Withdraw the total amount of assets from your RRSP or
3) Use the assets to purchase an annuity for life or
4) Use the assets to purchase an annuity spread over a number of years.

You can check with Revenue Canada yourself; but I recommend that you seek professional guidance from an investment advisor.

Let me leave you with this thought. After you pay for your home in full, instead of buying an RRSP you buy a more expensive home, but a home you can easily afford and still live within your means. In other words do not make yourself mortgage poor. (See chapter on buying a home).

If this new home were to earn 6% you would then earn 6% on a higher valued home, which means you will earn more money, tax-free.

When we die, Revenue Canada deems that we have disposed of all our assets on the day of our death. If you have a spouse or a significant other whom you live with (see Revenue Canada's definition for tax purposes) you are allowed to transfer all of your assets-tax free-to the surviving spouse. However, if there is no spouse, then all your assets are deemed to be disposed of at fair market value.

This includes all your RRSP monies, stocks, bonds, other property etc. What does this mean to those inheriting your wealth? It means everything will be taxed at your marginal tax rate for the year of your death.

Let's say for simplicity sake this marginal tax rate is 45%. This means that when you die and leave your RRSP's to your children, relatives or friends and they are worth $200,000.00 your estate must pay $90,000.00 in taxes before anyone get's anything.

Since your principle residence is free from tax it doesn't matter what its value is at the time of your death. If your home were worth $200,000.00 more because you bought a more expensive home instead of putting the money into an RRSP it would pass to your heirs' tax-free.

Investing to become wealthy is a lot easier than most people belief but getting there by investing only in your principal residence is not the best way. It is one way; but not the only way.

As with most assets, property values can and do go down in value and you may very well be in a down market, for real estate when you need the money the most. This is why I say "Never buy a home you can't afford."

There are many good investments to be invested in and I recommend that you diversify in a few different products such as stocks, bonds, cash and short term deposits; but talk to an investment advisor before making any investment decisions.

It is not my intention to give you advice on what you should invest in. My desire is to make you aware, that you have choices. Just because most people buy RRSP's doesn't necessarily make them the best investment choice. (*Speak to a investment advisor*).

❖

CHAPTER 28

United States of America Mortgage & Deed of Trust

What Is A Mortgage?

A mortgage (loan) is a security instrument used by the mortgagee (lender) and signed by the mortgagor (borrower). This instrument is publically recorded as a legal claim against the property. This instrument is issued alongside a promissory note. A promissory note is a legal document that you sign promising to pay back the money you borrowed from the lender to finance your home. There are two parties to this agreement the lender and the borrower.

What Is A Deed Of Trust?

A deed of trust is a legal instrument that is used in many U.S. states in lieu of a mortgage. It works similar to a mortgage in that it gives the lender a security interest in your property in case of default. This legal document has three parties.

They are:

Trustor:

This is the borrower.

Beneficiary:

This is the lender.

Trustee

This is the party that holds title to the property until you the Trustor finish making paying for the loan in full, sell the property or default (stop making your payments). A mortgage and a deed of trust are very similar to each other except in the case of you defaulting on the payments.

A deed of trust has a "power of sale clause" that is normally not found in a mortgage agreement. This enables the beneficiary (lender) to request the trustee, to sell the property by exercising the "power of sale clause". No lawsuit is required.

When a mortgage is used the mortgagee (lender) would in most cases need to file a lawsuit in order to foreclose on the property.

Different Kinds of Mortgages and Deeds Of trust

There are many different variations of mortgages and deeds of trust but in many cases they are similar to Canadian mortgages. The most popular ones from which you will make a choice are fixed rate of interest mortgages, adjustable rate mortgages (ARM), a combination of the two blended together. There is also Federal Housing Administration (FHA) mortgages.

Mortgage & Deed Of Trust Guidelines

Lenders under the Federal National Mortgage Association (Fannie May) or the Federal Home Loan Mortgage Corporation (Freddie Mac) are called "conforming lenders." These lenders follow the guidelines set out by the Federal National Mortgage Association.

These lenders lend to those borrowers, known as "A-paper borrowers". This means that the borrower could get a loan up to $417,000.00, on a single residence at an interest rate of about ¼% to ½% less than non A-paper borrowers.

All loans written by a conforming lender will require some type of private mortgage insurance (PMI) premium if the borrower's equity or down payment is less than 20%. This PMI insurance protects the lender in the event the borrower defaults. These loans are called conforming loans.

A non-conforming loan or jumbo loan is any loan for an amount greater than the maximum allowed under a conforming loan ($417,000.00). Please remember a non-conforming loan will cost ¼% to ½% more than the conforming loan.

Private Mortgage Insurance (PMI)

This insurance does not benefit the borrower in any way. It exists for the benefit of the lender. This insurance protects the lender in the unlikely event the borrower defaults on their payments.

This insurance is paid monthly and continues until you have between 20 to 22% equity in the home. Equity is the difference between the value of the home and the amount the borrower owes on it.

The cost of PMI varies according to the amount of equity you have in the home. If you have a down payment of 10 % you will pay approximately $45.00 a month for every $100,000.00 you borrow. This interest charge is not tax deductable.

❖

CHAPTER 29

United States Of America Mortgage And Deed Of Trust Options

In America you can take out a fixed loan rate mortgage for a 10, 15, 20, 25, 30, 35 or 40-year term and end the mortgage loan at any time by paying the loan in full. You can do this in most cases without paying any penalty. In essence this means that you have an open mortgage.

If you borrowed the money at a lower interest rate than the lenders are presently charging you would not want to pay the mortgage off unless you had the money to pay it in full or you were selling the property and moving.

Adjustable Rate Mortgages (ARM)

The ARM mortgage is best taken in periods of stable or declining interest rates or you plan on moving within a short period of time and most importantly you don't mind volatility.

The interest rate on these mortgages generally rises or falls, depending on the general market conditions. Most lenders tie their lending rate to the U.S. Treasury Bill index with a margin set approximately two basis points above the Treasury rate. Normally the rate is set for a certain period of time such as 12-months to as long as a couple of years and then it adjusts to fixed market rates.

However, make sure if you choose this method to finance your property that you have a ceiling cap on how much the lender can increase the rate of interest they will charge you. Oftentimes there is a yearly and or lifetime cap. Please be careful because there have been instances where the lender has raised interest rates as much as 6% more than the original rate they have charged.

You must be careful with an ARM mortgage, especially if interest rates increase but your payments remain the same.

Why should you care if interest rates increase?

Because if the interest rate increases and your payment doesn't you may find yourself in a negative situation. You may owe more at the end of the mortgage term than when you started.

Anyone taking this type of mortgage must pay attention to what is happening to his or her rate. If you are not prepared to stay on top of what happens then I recommend that you go with a fixed rate. With a fixed rate you at least know that the payment has been matched to the interest cost and the term of the mortgage.

Fixed Rate Mortgage

These types of mortgages are the most popular available. The rate is stable and does not change until the agreed upon term is completed. These mortgages are best taken when rates are low and you think they will be increasing. Also, great if you don't like volatility or are on a fixed income, plan to retire within a few years and need that extra stability.

Term, is the length of time, it will take for you to pay the mortgage in full. Term length can be short or long but the most common length is 20, 25 or 30-years. The mortgage payment is preset at a level you can afford. For example, if you were to borrow $200,000.00 at a 6% interest rate for 30 years your monthly payment would be approximately $1,200.00 per month. However, if you were to pay the mortgage over 25-years the monthly payment would be approximately $1,300.00 per month.

Blended Mortgage

This is a fixed and adjustable rate mortgage combined into one. For example if you have a 30-year mortgage, you could have the first few years as an adjustable rate mortgage and the remaining years at a fixed rate. Keep in mind that you could also have it the other way around whereby you have a fixed rate for the first few years and then an adjustable rate mortgage.

Federal Housing Administration (FHA)

The FHA offers mortgages in the range of approximately $200,000.00 to $362,800.00 for a single family dwelling, depending on where the property is located. The FHA is a division of the federal government and they may be willing to give you a mortgage even if you once had a bad credit rating.

❖

CHAPTER 30

United States Of America Prepayment Privileges

Prepayment Privileges

This chapter is similar to the Canadian prepayment privileges shown in Chapter 21. However, the good news is that you do not have the penalties that Canadians have.

Three Different Ways to Prepay

1) Lump Sum Payment
2) Increase your payment amount
3) Make your payments more often

Lump Sum

Most lenders will allow you to make a lump sum payment on your mortgage once a year. You must check with your lender to find out how much of a prepayment they will allow. Also check to find out how much notice they require in order to process your request. Most likely it will be the equivalent of ones months' payment per year. However, please do not assume this, check with the lender.

Increased Payment Amount

This is not widely available but usually the major lenders will allow you to increase your payment amount. Again, check with you lender to see if you are allowed to do this. Don't ask them if they think it is a good idea ask if you are allowed the reason I say this is you don't want them to try to discourage you from doing this.

Why would they to do this?

They would do it because if you increase the payment amount you will cut down the amount of interest they will earn.

Make The Payments More Often

When you increase the frequency of your payments you start saving the amount of interest you would pay immediately. Not only will you save on your interest cost you will save on the length of time it will take you to pay the loan in full.

If you were to change the payment frequency to every 2-weeks you would need to take your monthly payment and divide it by 2. If your monthly mortgage payment were $700.00 per month, divide it by 2 and your new payment would become $350.00 every 2-weeks. Now multiply this by 26 and you get $9,100.00 of mortgage payments per year.

A year of monthly mortgage payments' would total $8,400.00. So, by paying every 2-weeks you would pay an extra $700.00 per year. These extra payments would save you money on your interest cost and reduce your principal amount by the $700.00 plus a little extra because of the interest savings.

CHAPTER 31

❖

United States of America Portable Mortgage

A portable mortgage is a mortgage that you can take with you from one home to another.

This portable mortgage option does not make a great deal of sense in America for a couple of reasons. The first reason is that you will pay a premium interest rate on the loan of approximately ½%. Remember this premium is for the term of the mortgage.

If you have a 30-year fixed rate term mortgage, you will be paying this premium for the entire term of the loan.

The second point is, if you don't have sufficient money you will need to borrow more. You could take a home equity loan or arrange for a second mortgage; both of these options are costly. Another option is to cancel out the old portable loan and get a new loan for the amount of money you would be borrowing. In this case you would have paid the loan premium for portability and not received any benefit.

Portability makes a lot of sense when you know you will be moving in less than 5-years and you will not require any more money. This most likely will occur when you are downsizing your home or when you know of any money you may receive such as a bonus or inheritance.

CHAPTER 32

❖

Closing Comments

The world of investing, finance and taxation is very complicated and the rules are constantly changing. I strongly recommend that before you do anything; consult with a professional advisor for expert advice on what plan of action would be best suited for you.

Open any newspaper and look at the mess that the market is in at the present time and not just here in North America but globally.

Be sure to always ask your advisor at least the following questions.

"What risk am I taking?"

"Am I insured against possible loss?"

"Are you personally invested in this product?'

"What do you know personally about this investment and the people who are running the company?"

Have they fully read the prospectus, if they have, ask them to explain it to you. It will help you understand if they understand it and it will help you, when you read it.

Ask the advisor to explain in detail why they feel this is the best product for you.

Also, be sure to ask what fees they charge. There are many different fee structures. A few funds do not charge any fees but most do charge and some charge plenty.

Mutual Fund/Hedge funds often charge a 2% management fee, plus up to a 20% performance fee, if they reach a certain performance level as outlined in the agreement. This 20% charge kicks in whenever the fund beats a predetermined percentage return or by beating a benchmark index.

If they should lose money in a given period, usually a one year period then they only charge the 2% management fee. Sometimes depending on the agreement it would be necessary for the fund to achieve their highest peak in value as set out in the agreement before they can start to charge the 20% again.

It is important for you to know the management's track record because a few hedge fund managers will close out a losing fund and start a new fund, rather than wait to beat the level they need to beat before they start earning their performance bonus again. And some agreements allow the management to start anew after 2-years if they haven't beaten the high point. In other words, they start again after the 2-year time frame and get the 20% without them having to beat their high point.

Not all funds are created equally so check before you agree to commit your money!

I do hope you have enjoyed reading this book as much as I have enjoyed writing it. If you put the information I have given you to practical use and put it to use now, you will surely succeed in your financial goals and sooner than you ever thought possible.

I am positively certain that if you adopt only a few of my many examples you will increase your net-worth substantially.

Appendix:

Expense Heading

Date of Expense	What you Purchased	QTY	Cost Each	Total Cost

Credit Card Listing

Name of Card Company	Interest Rate	Amount Owing	Minimum Pymt.

Credit Card Cancellation Letter

[Your name]
[Your address]

[Date]

To Whom It May Concern:
RE: Closing my credit card

Please let this letter serve as notice that effective immediately, I am closing and terminating my credit card account and any and all accounts that are guaranteed by me.

This closure is not a result of anything you or your company has done, but is simply a necessary step in my financial planning.

[Name on credit card]
[Account number]
[Account expiry date]

Please send to me written confirmation that my account has been closed. Also, please confirm that you have notified all appropriate credit card bureaus that this account was closed at my request.

Thank you for your prompt attention to this matter.

Yours truly,

[Your signature]

[Your Name]